Taxation of Lloyd's Under

Taxation of Lloyd's Underwriters

Second Edition

K. S. Carmichael CBE, FCA, FTII
(Longcrofts)

and

P. H. Wolstenholme MA, FCA
(Spicer and Pegler)

THE INSTITUTE OF
CHARTERED
ACCOUNTANTS

IN ENGLAND & WALES

Butterworths/HFL
in association with
The Institute of Chartered Accountants
in England and Wales
1985

United Kingdom	Butterworth & Co (Publishers) Ltd, 88 Kingsway, LONDON WC2B 6AB and 61A North Castle Street, EDINBURGH EH2 3LJ
Australia	Butterworths Pty Ltd, SYDNEY, MELBOURNE, BRISBANE, ADELAIDE, PERTH, CANBERRA and HOBART
Canada	Butterworth & Co (Canada) Ltd, TORONTO and VANCOUVER
New Zealand	Butterworths of New Zealand Ltd, WELLINGTON and AUCKLAND
Singapore	Butterworth & Co (Asia) Pte Ltd, SINGAPORE
South Africa	Butterworth Publishers (Pty) Ltd, DURBAN and PRETORIA
USA	Butterworth Legal Publishers, ST PAUL, Minnesota, SEATTLE, Washington, BOSTON, Massachusetts, AUSTIN, Texas and D & S Publishers, CLEARWATER, Florida

First edition 1980

© C. K. S. Carmichael and P. H. Wolstenholme 1985

British Library cataloguing in publication data
Carmichael, K. S.
    Taxation of Lloyd's underwriters.—2nd ed.
    1. Lloyd's of London   2. Syndicates (Finance)—
    Great Britain   3. Insurance—Taxation—Great
    Britain
    I. Title   II. Wolstenholme, Peter
    336.24′24   HG8039

    ISBN 0 406 67880 4

Photoset by Cotswold Typesetting Ltd, Cheltenham
Printed and bound by Biddles Ltd, Guildford, Surrey

The purpose of this book

This book is not a history of Lloyd's nor an exposition of the detailed tax computations of the individual syndicates. Its purpose is to assist underwriting members and their professional advisers to deal with the taxation of a member's income.

Due to the particular needs of Lloyd's, its importance in the financial life of the United Kingdom and the complexities of insurance, the taxation provisions relating to its activities are complex. Accounts are kept open for two years following the end of a particular calendar year so as to take account, so far as possible, of all claims in respect of the premiums received in that year. This means that the underwriting member has an open tax position for at least three years.

An individual member or his professional accountant should be able, by using this book in conjunction with the various documents and returns which will be received, to determine his final tax bill on the income of a particular calendar year. The book is a working manual. The effect of other taxes will be dealt with only so far as it is necessary to explain the position regarding Lloyd's.

Before going into this matter further, there is a preliminary chapter on the requirements of Lloyd's as to financial stability etc., so that the reader is led through from the point at which a person decides to become an underwriting member of Lloyd's to the point of death.

The Lloyd's tax forms, of which specimens are shown, are Crown Copyright and the permission of the Controller of Her Majesty's Stationery Office to reproduce them is gratefully acknowledged.

K. S. CARMICHAEL
P. H. WOLSTENHOLME
117 Newberries Ave
Radlett, Herts
56–60 St Mary Axe
London EC3A 8BJ

Contents

Contents

Glossary of terms

Underwriting Member

Any person elected to Underwriting Membership of Lloyd's and subscribing to Lloyd's policies issued in accordance with the Insurance Companies' Acts and complying with the regulations for membership as laid down by the Council of Lloyd's.

Name

An Underwriting Member whose name appears on the list of those participating in any Syndicate at Lloyd's is known as a 'Name' on that syndicate.

Active Underwriter

The person (usually, but not necessarily, an underwriting Member) who conducts underwriting on behalf of a Syndicate of Underwriting Members.

Underwriting Agent at Lloyd's

An individual person, firm or company having complied with the requirements of the Council of Lloyd's for conducting an Underwriting Agency at Lloyd's. Whilst a list of Underwriting Agents is not published, the Membership Department at Lloyd's can confirm to potential candidates whether a specific person, firm or company is on the list of Agents.

Co-ordinating Agent

A Name underwriting under more than one Underwriting Agent is required to nominate one of his Agents for co-ordinating his Premium Limits; the Agent so nominated will be responsible for keeping the Council informed how the Name's

Premium Income will be allocated. The Co-ordinating Agent is also responsible for handling matters leading up to the Name's election, once the Council of Lloyd's has agreed that the application may go forward.

Underwriting Agency Agreement

The contract entered into by an Underwriting Member with the Underwriting Agent or Agents selected by him to conduct a class or classes of business underwritten at Lloyd's. Whilst there are certain provisions common to all Underwriting Agency Agreements, the individual Agency terms, as regards the charging of the Underwriting Salary, the Profit Commission and the manner in which these items are charged to the Name, vary as between individual Agents and there is no standard form common to all Agencies at Lloyd's.

General Undertaking

This document, which must be signed by each Candidate for Membership, supplements the Regulations contained in Lloyd's Acts and Byelaws and imposes obligations which bind a Member during the whole course of his Underwriting. A copy of the General Undertaking is given to each Candidate soon after his application for Membership is received by the Council.

Premiums Trust Fund

It is a requirement of the Insurance Companies Acts that all premiums and other underwriting monies and the investment thereof shall at all times be placed and held in trust under a Premiums Trust Deed in a form prescribed by the Council of Lloyd's with the prior approval of the Department of Trade and Industry. This Premiums Trust Fund is held in the names of not less than two Trustees or may be held to the order of such Trustees by any nominee Company approved for such purpose by the Council of Lloyd's. Payment is made out of this fund of claims, expenses and, ultimately to the Member, of profits on closed underwriting accounts.

Lloyd's Deposits

Investments or cash held in the sole name of the Corporation of Lloyd's as Trustee for an individual Underwriting Member under a Deposit Trust Deed executed by the Member and on which the Member or beneficial owner is entitled to receive the dividends and interest. The Deposit consists of:

(a) A basic Deposit
(b) A Premium Income Deposit, the amount of which determines the overall Premium Limit for the Member;
(c) Additional Deposit required in respect of residence outside the United Kingdom.

Although the Lloyd's Deposit is transferred into the name of the Corporation and held by the Council, it is not the responsibility of the Council or the Council staff to advise upon the securities selected or to be selected except to ensure that the securities are acceptable according to Council rules. The responsibility for the investments in the Deposit rests, within the Rules laid down by the Council, with the individual Member. If the Member wishes to delegate the investment of his Deposit to his Underwriting Agent he may do so, but, in this event, written notice to this effect must be given to the Manager of the Membership Department. Lloyd's Names may have their deposit provided by their employer or immediate family, where they work in Lloyd's. In such cases the employer etc. must enter into an 'undertaking not to claim' as well as becoming a party to the Deposit Trust Deed.

Premium Limit

The permissible total amount of Premium Income which may be underwritten by an individual Name in any one calendar year in the Syndicates in which he underwrites. The Premium Limit is an overall Limit which is allocated to Syndicates in proportions agreed by the Name in consultation with his Underwriting Agent or Agents and it is upon such overall Limit that the Premium Income Deposit is based.

With the approval of the Underwriting Agent or Agents concerned, a Name may request the Council of Lloyd's to grant him an increase in his overall Premium Limit. Such increased Limit is granted subject both to satisfactory evidence of Means and to the Provision of the necessary additional Deposits.

An increase in the overall Premium Limit may also be granted consequent upon appreciation in the total Market Value of the Lloyd's Deposit. In this event the new Premium Limit may be based on the appreciated value of the Deposit with the approval of the Name and the Agent or Agents concerned. On the other hand, subsequent depreciation could have the effect if fairly substantial, of reducing the permitted overall Premium Limit.

Any Name who exceeds his permitted overall Limit may be required to increase his Deposits to cover such excess.

Nomination Form

When issued by the Council, the Sponsor and one other Member of Lloyd's are required to sign this form recommending the candidate as suitable for election. The completed forms are then posted in a conspicuous place on the Notice Board in the Underwriting Room at Lloyd's for seven days.

Entrance Fee

The cash payment to the Corporation of Lloyd's on election as an Underwriting Member based on the classes of business to be underwritten in the year following that of election.

The Entrance Fee is varied according to the classes of business underwritten and the category of Membership qualification. If, with the approval of the Council additional classes of business are commended at a later date, then additional contributions to the Corporation funds may be payable.

For taxation purposes Entrance Fees are analogous to the formation expenses of a business and, as such, are treated as capital payments and cannot be deducted from underwriting profits for tax purposes as an expense of the business.

Lloyd's Special Reserve Funds

After their election all Names are asked by their Agents whether they wish to participate in the Special Reserve Fund Scheme. This Scheme enables a Member to place part of his underwriting profits to reserve with certain tax advantages. The funds can only be withdrawn for the payment of an overall underwriting loss, or on death or resignation. Full details of the Scheme are set out in an explanatory memorandum, which is usually forwarded by the Agent.

'General', 'Ordinary', or 'Personal' Reserve Fund of the Name

Under the terms of most Underwriting Agency Agreements, the Underwriting Agent has authority to retain part or all of the profits of a Name, in addition to amounts put to the Special Reserve Fund, when it is deemed prudent to increase reserves.

Lloyd's Audit

The annual Audit of the Underwriting Accounts of each Underwriting Member of Lloyd's conducted by an approved Auditor on the Lloyd's Panel of Auditors under the Audit Instructions issued to each Auditor and to all Underwriting Agents as at 31 December of every year.

Audit Reserves

The amount which at 31 December of each year of underwriting must remain in credit against each main class of business transacted by a Name, to meet the estimated cost (based on the Lloyd's Audit formula) of winding-up the Name's Underwriting Accounts.

Reinsurance to Close

The method by which the outstanding liability on the Underwriting Account of a Lloyd's Syndicate for any one year of Account is closed (usually, but not necessarily, at the end of its third year) by reinsuring such liability into the Account of a later Underwriting Year.

A reinsurance premium is charged to the Underwriting Account of the closing year and credited to that of the reinsuring year, which then adds to its liabilities a sum equal to the reinsurance premium so received and pays all claims which would otherwise be the liability of the Underwriting Year so reinsured.

Closed Years

An Underwriting Account of a Syndicate which has been debited with a reinsurance premium to close the Account (referred to above) is known as a 'Closed' Account, and the profits (or losses) thereon are then apportionable to the Names participating therein.

Lloyd's Central Fund

A fund established in 1926 to protect Policyholders in case any Underwriting Member should be unable to meet his liabilities out of his Syndicate Trust Funds, his funds deposited at Lloyd's, his Reserves and personal assets outside Lloyd's.

Each member, on election, agrees to be bound by the Agreement constituting the Fund and to pay the annual scale contributions thereto. These contributions are usually paid by the Agent(s) concerned and debited to the Personal Account of the Name.

Lloyd's Charities Trust

A charitable fund, approved by the Inland Revenue, to which all Members are invited to donate under Deeds of Covenant. The fund is administered by the Council of Lloyd's as Trustees, and its main purpose is to make donations to deserving charities of a national character, Mansion House appeals and other appeals which commend themselves to the Trustees. The amount paid (together with the tax thereon at the basic rate) is deductible in determining the higher and up to 1983–84 additional rate taxes of the Name.

Lloyd's Benevolent Fund

A charitable fund voluntarily contributed to by Members and administered by the Trustees for the benefit of persons connected with Lloyd's, or their dependants, who fall on difficult times.

Working Name

An underwriter who spends at least 75 per cent of his normal working week engaged in the room or in the office of an underwriting agent.

Underwriting Account

The Syndicate's accounts drawn up for a trading year, which is the calendar year.

1 Joining Lloyd's

The organisation of Lloyd's

1.1 The Corporation of Lloyd's ('Lloyd's') was incorporated by statute in 1871 and its affairs are regulated under the Lloyd's Acts 1871–1982. The 1982 Act completely reorganised the administration of Lloyds. Under it the Council is given extensive powers to regulate the activities of brokers and agents and to provide more information to Names. Following the passing of the Act, the Council have issued byelaws which provide regulations covering disciplinary procedures, investigations, appointment of committees, the accounts to be presented to Names and the audit of syndicates. The purpose is to provide information to Names and to show to outsiders the high standards required of those involved with Lloyds. Its function is to provide the premises in which Members meet to transact business and to provide the necessary administrative and clerical services and aids to facilitate underwriting; overall supervision of the annual audit of Members' accounts; and advice concerning foreign legislation and tax. The general direction of the Corporation is under a Council of 28 Members, comprising 16 writing, 8 external and 4 nominated members.

1.2 Although Members join together into a group to do business (known as a syndicate) each underwrites a risk in his own name, with unlimited liability. The liability is several and not joint. Syndicate Members are not in partnership. This legal position has a material effect on the accounting procedures and tax liability.

1.3 Syndicates at Lloyd's are divided broadly into four divisions, namely Marine, Non-Marine, Motor and Aviation. Broadly, the Marine syndicate deals with shipping, the Motor with motor insurance, the Aviation with aviation insurance and the Non-Marine with anything else. It is usual for a person to join a number of syndicates and the extent to which he divides his interest between marine, non-marine, motor and aviation, while a personal choice, is usually guided by the underwriting agents. There are a number of specialised syndicates, e.g. livestock.

1.4. When a person wishes to become a Lloyd's underwriter ('Member' or 'Name'), he must find an existing Member to sponsor him usually by 30 June preceding the proposed first year. Before anybody can become a Member, there is a detailed investigation of his affairs. If valuable time is not to be wasted, sponsors will recommend only people they have known for several years and of whom they have a high regard as to their financial stability. The sponsoring Member usually arranges for the prospective Member to meet his own Underwriting Agents. The underwriting agent for each syndicate has complete control concerning each Member's activities, the risks he underwrites, the rate of premiums charged, the claims accepted and their settlement, the investment of premiums received during the three years the account is open and of the Member's reserves and the preparation of his accounts. The efficiency of the agent is a material factor in determining the Member's profit or loss. A prospective Member should study the past results, which the agent will disclose to him, and discuss the investment policy applicable to the syndicate. He must decide whether he wishes to be represented by one of the larger firms of underwriting agents, one of the smaller or one of the newer or recently set up agencies. He should remember that the level at which reinsurance of risks occurs affects profits but reduces the risk. A substantial part of the return is frequently represented by the interest and dividends arising from the investment of the premiums, mostly in short-dated government stocks.

The agent will be interested in the means of the prospective Name. He must show wealth of not less than £100,000 (Lloyds Vocational Names have their limits fixed by having to provide means equal to a percentage of their premium limit). Each additional Name in a syndicate enables that syndicate to take additional premium income and consequently increases the possibility of profit or loss. The addition of a Name with assets of £75,000 permits the syndicate to write a further £150,000 of premium income in the year, i.e. the ratio of premium income to wealth is two to one. A working party has suggested this be amended so that the means equal 40 per cent of the gross overall premium limit. With inflation, the number of Members in each syndicate has had to be increased or existing Members would have to increase their commitment if the same volume of risks is to be insured, but an increase in the number of Members means profits are divided over a greater number of persons. Existing Names wish to maintain their income, so the relationship between the total premium limits of the syndicate and the number of Names is of interest.

Where the proposed Name is employed by an underwriting agent or a Lloyd's broker and is a UK resident, he may be admitted as Lloyd's Vocational Names on being supported by his firm.

A spouse is entitled to join on 1 January following a member's death if agreed with the underwriting agent during the member's lifetime on complying with the current means test and providing a Lloyd's deposit. The application must be made before 1 December for UK residents and 1 November for those overseas.

The certificate of means

1.5 A prospective Name must provide details of his assets and liabilities in a statement, referred to as a Certificate of Means. This is completed by either his banker, solicitor or accountant. The certificate is unlikely to include all of the prospective Name's assets, for some are not acceptable at Lloyd's. The acceptable assets are:

(a) *not less than 60 per cent of means*: cash, at bank or building society;
(b) stock exchange-quoted stocks and shares, except no one security can be included to an extent greater than 30 per cent of means;
(c) life policies at surrender value;
(d) reversionary absolute interests in trust at actuarial value;
(e) bank guarantees or letters of credit;
(f) gold (limited to 30 per cent of means and only 70 per cent of value is allowed) in form of bullion or coins held at approved bank; and *not more than 40 per cent of means*;
(g) Barclays Bank guarantee covered by a counter indemnity provided by the Sun Alliance Insurance Group on works of art pledged as security. The guarantee will be normally for 35 per cent of the total valuation;
(h) real property at market value;
(i) leasehold property if the age of the applicant and the unexpired period of the lease total at least 100 years with a minimum unexpired period of 50 years.

3

1.6 Although land and buildings are acceptable assets, the private residence cannot be included. Shares must be in UK companies with issued capital of at least £1m, on which dividends have been paid for 5 years and are officially quoted. Authorised unit trust, government stocks and national savings certificates may be included.

1.7 Shares in private companies, livestock, loans to individuals or companies, mortgages, yachts, jewellery and motor cars, interests in partnerships and other personal effects are not acceptable. If these have to be included to meet the minimum limit, the prospective Name obtains a letter of credit or bank guarantee secured on them.

1.8 The assets must be owned directly by the prospective Name. It is not possible to include interests in discretionary trusts since these do not belong to him. Similarly, a wife's assets cannot be treated as belonging to the husband or vice versa. If a person by some voluntary act reduces his assets below £100,000 he must inform the Council who may require him to cease underwriting. Certain employees in the insurance industry are sponsored by their employers, who provide the assets on loan or provide a bank guarantee.

The general undertaking etc.

1.9 The means test having been satisfied, the candidate does nothing. A nomination form signed by the sponsor and one other Member is posted on the Notice Board in the Underwriting Room. In due time, the prospective Member, through his agent, is asked to attend before the rota committee. Members of this committee satisfy themselves that the prospective Member—

(a)　is aware he will be trading with unlimited liability;

(b)　has been made aware of the past results of the syndicates he is joining;

(c)　has been supplied with satisfactory answers to all questions raised; and

(d)　has supplied correct information as to means.

1.10 Having satisfied the rota committee, the prospective Member signs certain forms. These forms are:

(a)　an 'assignment of premium' form;

(b) a 'security' form;
(c) an 'application for a social security number to the United States Government'; and
(d) a general undertaking.

1.11 The 'assignment of premiums' form provides that the Name assigns to the Society of Lloyd's all premium income and permits the Society to hold the money on trust to meet all claims on policies which are written by the Name. It enables him to carry on the business through Lloyd's but does not create any trust for the purposes of either capital gains tax or capital transfer tax.

1.12 The 'security' form lists the assets which it is proposed to provide for the purposes of Lloyd's deposit. Each underwriting member must deposit with Lloyd's a basic deposit of in the case of UK, EEC, and Commonwealth citizens resident and domiciled in the UK, 25% of the premium income (minimum, £12,500); for such persons resident or domiciled outside the UK, 30% of the premium income (minimum £22,500); and other Nationals, wherever resident, 35% of the premium income (minimum, £26,250). The deposits may be invested in securities of the Member's choice (and may include certain life policies) provided that these are acceptable to the Lloyd's Council. Frequently the underwriting agent manages the deposit. The deposit may consist of cash or narrower-range or wider-range investments, or any combination thereof, providing at least 25% is in cash or dated British Government securities repayable within 5 years. Narrower-range investments are those defined in the Trustee Investments Act 1961, with certain exceptions. Wider-range investments cannot include shares in a company with an issued capital of less than £1m and a market value of £1m or less. The deposit of an overseas resident must be provided by a bank guarantee or letter of credit. While this security suits Lloyds, it avoids capital transfer tax on the amount of the deposit. Bearer bonds or securities are not acceptable. The actual certificates for the stocks and shares held on a Lloyd's deposit are retained in the custody of the Council of Lloyd's.

1.13 When assigning the form of security it is necessary to satisfy Lloyd's that none of the assets can be made liable for capital transfer tax. Accordingly, the candidate has to sign a certificate as follows:

5

Capital Transfer Tax

The Finance Act 1975 provides that the holder of assets where ownership has been transferred by way of a gift can be made liable for capital transfer tax.

As it is essential that Lloyd's deposits should not be liable, each owner of the proposed securities is required to sign one of the following declarations:

(1) I confirm that no part of the proposed securities has been received by way of gift since 25 March 1974

Signed ....

(2) The proposed securities have been received in whole or in part by way of gift since 25 March 1974 and I confirm that any capital transfer tax in respect of such a gift has been provided for

Signed ....

United States questionnaire

1.14 As a substantial part of Lloyd's income arises from insurances in America, a Name must complete a 'United States Federal income tax questionnaire'. Completion and filing gives him a social security number. Members of Lloyd's are deemed to have a permanent establishment in the United States for the purposes of United States Federal income tax and must file income tax returns. The questionnaire contains the following questions:

A (1) Of what country are you a citizen?
(2) What country, if any, issued your passport?
(3) Were you ever a United States citizen?
(4) Please state the country of which you are resident for tax purposes.

B (1) Name and address of person filing United States income tax returns on your behalf
(this part is only completed if the person is already filing United States tax returns in which case Part A need not be completed).
(2) Your tax identification (United States social security number).

1.15 Where a person has not previously filed United States income tax returns an application for a social security number must be completed. This requires the following details:

(a) the Name's full name, including christian names;
(b) the full name given at birth;
(c) the place of birth, showing the city and country;
(d) the Name's mother's full name at her birth;
(e) the Name's father's full name;
(f) whether or not an application has previously been made for a United States social security, railroad or tax account number;
(g) the date of birth;
(h) the present age on last birthday;
(i) the sex;
(j) colour or race;
(k) telephone number of the person signing; and
(l) his signature and the date of signing.

The last two forms will authorise United States attorneys to file returns on behalf of the Name. Annually a Name must complete a form by February 15 which he sends to his underwriting agent for onward despatch to Lloyd's American attorneys. The latter file the details with the Internal Revenue Service.

1.16 The general undertaking binds a Name to act in conjunction with the Council of Lloyd's in connection with any claims made, to have his accounts properly audited and to agree to abide by certain agreements which have been made by Lloyd's for the general benefit of members and insured persons, such as those relating to the Central Guarantee Fund, the provision of security through Additional Securities Ltd, and the arrangements with the Lloyd's Policy Signing Office. In effect, by signing the undertaking, the prospective Member agrees to abide by and act in accordance with a course of conduct laid down by the Council.

Election day

1.17 The foregoing forms being completed, the Council of Lloyd's elect the applicant as an underwriting member of Lloyd's from 1 January in a calendar year. Upon election an entrance fee of £3,000 is payable unless working at Lloyds. Assuming the underwriting agent makes profits on behalf of the Name, the entrance fee is the only cash sum which is actually paid away throughout the whole of the underwriting career except perhaps for the first annual subscription. To avoid any loss of this sum, the Name can take out life insurance for that amount and designate a relative as the recipient of the insurance monies. As the premiums are payable out of income the arrangement has the effect of passing assets to the relative without any capital transfer tax or capital gains tax liability, while ensuring that the family does not lose if the Name dies before the profits exceed the amount of the entrance fee.

1.18 Each underwriting member pays an annual subscription to the Corporation of Lloyd's. Apart from the first year, when it is usually paid by the Name to the underwriting agent, who passes it on to the Council, the agent pays the subscription and deducts it from the Name's share of profits. The annual subscription is allowable for tax purposes. Relief will be automatically obtained when it is paid by the agent; particular care must be taken to obtain relief for the first annual subscription paid by the Name. Once the election has taken place, and the deposit and first year subscription are paid, the Name does not enjoy any profits for a period of three years.

2 The first three years

Income from Lloyd's deposit

2.1 During the first three calendar years of membership, the underwriter does not receive profits from the underwriting syndicates. Each underwriting account is kept open for a period of not less than three years. During that period, the underwriting agent receives premiums on behalf of the syndicate members, meets claims and suffers administrative charges. The premiums are invested, usually in government securities, and the Name does not have any direct interest therein. He is interested only in the capital gains arising on the investment of his deposit and the income from this deposit.

2.2 As indicated earlier, the securities comprising the deposit are held in the name of the Council of Lloyd's. Effectively, they are the first fund out of which to meet any claims in excess of the premiums received. The transfer into the name of the Council is not a disposal for capital gains tax or capital transfer tax purposes, unlike other transfers to a trust. Although the securities are held in trust, for tax purposes the Name is deemed to hold the securities in his own name and under his own control. Accordingly, he is responsible for the tax on any capital gains made and any income received.

2.3 The capital gain on any disposal of a security originally transferred to form part of the deposit is determined by reference to the original cost of the security to the Name or its value at 6 April 1965, and not by reference to the value at the date of the transfer to Lloyd's. The gain on investments acquired out of a cash deposit or out of the proceeds of sale of securities originally deposited with Lloyd's is calculated by reference to cost. As this book is aimed at those who joined subsequent to 1975, such securities must have been acquired since 6 April 1965.

2.4 The income arising from the deposit is mandated by the

9

underwriting agent to the Name's bank account. Care is needed where the investments comprising the deposit are managed by the underwriting agent. Usually, the agent provides a schedule of dividends received during each tax year but that schedule may not include all income received. Where the Name has transferred securities to form the deposit and these are not within the usual list adopted by the Name, the income therefrom may not appear on the schedule. The Name or his agent should check with the bank account.

Example

The managing agents might provide a schedule of dividends paid during a particular year as follows:

NAME OF UNDERWRITER	SCHEME DIVIDENDS PAID DURING 1984–85		
Stock	*Date paid*	*Dividend*	*Interest*
Barclays Bank Ltd	21.4.84	23.64	
Royal Insurance Co Ltd	19.5.84	198.70	
Dunlop Holdings Ltd	3.7.84	53.00	
Whitbread & Co Ltd	21.7.84	55.80	
3 per cent Treasury Stock 1985	17.9.84		105.52
Barclays Bank Ltd	2.10.84	25.41	
Treasury 9 per cent 1994	17.11.84		30.15
Dunlop Holdings Ltd	2.1.85	53.00	
Royal Insurance Co Ltd	2.1.85	148.50	
Whitbread & Co Ltd	11.1.85	26.40	
3 per cent Treasury Stock 1985	21.5.85		105.53

The Name may have transferred as part of his deposit shares in Cadbury Schweppes and the Electra Investment Trust. As these are not securities within the usual list, they may not appear on the form. The taxpayer must pick up dividends on such holdings and include them in his tax return of income. They constitute income justifying the transfer to Special Reserve Fund (see **5.3**).

2.5 Any funds not invested in income-earning securities are placed on bank deposit in a central group account. Interest thereon, received without deduction of tax, is taxed directly on the Name. The Name receives a notice directly from Lloyd's. Such interest is assessed by the Name's Inspector of Taxes and not by the Underwriting Unit at Leeds. The latter deals with assessments on Lloyd's income. The address is Kingswood House, Richard-Shaw Lane, Pudsey LS28 6BM (tel: 0532-562256).

2.6 Having received the schedules from the underwriting agent or prepared them from his own bank statements, the figures are included on the Name's tax return in the normal way. They should be marked as relating to a Lloyd's deposit, unless the Name has already been supplied with the special income tax return for Lloyd's underwriters, when they are included in the appropriate section of the form.

Accounts

2.7 Approximately four months after the end of each calendar year the syndicate accounts are distributed to the Names. On a Name joining on 1 January 1983, a typical balance sheet and underwriting account appears as follows:

Example

BALANCE SHEET 31 DECEMBER 1983

	1983 £	1982 £
OPEN UNDERWRITING ACCOUNTS		
Underwriting account balances		
1982 account	9,574,644	11,612,958
1983 account	4,873,180	6,049,762
	14,447,824	17,662,720
Less members' personal expenses		
1982 account	205,546	173,102
1983 account	261,906	212,504
	467,452	385,606
	£13,980,372	£17,277,114
Represented by net assets		
Cash at bank	494,682	578,470
Deposit with Additional Securities Ltd	174,835	181,570
Foreign currency held by Lloyd's	943,886	1,511,032
Brokers' balances and other debtors	3,027,579	3,486,594
Investments at market value		
Sterling government stocks	4,110,315	4,533,948
equities	208,307	206,742
USA government stocks	5,676,921	7,915,942
equities	393,791	241,500
Canada government stocks	320,160	360,024
equities	100,726	6,272
	15,451,202	19,022,094
Less Members' personal accounts	1,029,267	1,242,494
Sundry creditors	441,563	502,486
	1,470,830	1,744,980
	£13,980,372	£17,277,114

Example **2.7**

OPEN UNDERWRITING ACCOUNTS AT 31 DECEMBER 1983

1982 account to end of second year

	1983	1981 account
	£	£
Net premiums	8,129,242	8,060,243
Net claims	3,720,410	3,226,480
	4,408,832	4,833,763
Reinsurance of 1981 account	5,130,052	6,716,692
Gross underwriting balance	9,538,884	11,550,455
Less: syndicate expenses	295,400	204,247
	9,243,484	11,346,208
Add: interest (net)	110,740	102,400
appreciation of investments (gross)	220,420	164,350
Balance held subject to further claims etc.	£9,574,644	£11,612,958

1983 account to end of first year

	1983	1982 account
	£	£
Net premiums	5,797,505	7,070,487
Net claims	720,271	896,721
Gross underwriting balance	5,077,234	6,173,766
Less: syndicate expenses	317,204	221,750
	4,760,030	5,952,016
Add: interest (net)	38,950	45,126
appreciation of investments (gross)	74,200	52,620
Balance held subject to further claims	£4,873,180	£6,049,762

2.7 The first three years

SYNDICATE EXPENSES AT 31 DECEMBER 1983

	1981 account	1982 account	1983 account	1980 account
	£	£	£	£
Audit	7,282	3,920	5,140	6,150
Computer	7,200	7,400	3,500	7,000
Printing and Stationery	742	691	746	520
Rent & office services	20,510	21,240	29,420	17,430
Salaries	117,731	169,814	220,443	117,117
Seats & substitutes	8,245	8,610	9,100	7,500
Signing Bureau charges	71,560	70,300	31,400	40,400
Subscriptions	3,200	4,150	5,240	2,875
Sundries	5,130	9,275	12,215	4,950
	£241,600	£295,400*	£317,204	£203,942†

Notes:
1 The figures are cumulative so that the figure for the 1981 account is the total of all expenses incurred in respect of that account during the three years it is open.
2 *This figure, representing the expenses incurred to the end of the second year of the 1982 account, is found in the open account for that year.
3 A major part of the expenses for any account are incurred in the first year. The writing of the insurance, collection of premiums and the receipt of claims mostly occurs in that period. Subsequent expenditure covers the 'cleaning up' process.
4 †This figure appeared in the 1980 account when closed.

Notes

(1) As an underwriting account is kept open for three years, during the first two years in which a person is interested, he is not entitled to any underwriting profits.

(2) If he joined on 1 January 1983, he receives a copy of the accounts and balance sheet made up to 31 December 1983, incorporating the balances on the 1982 and 1983 accounts because these are still open at that time. The balances represent the difference between the premium received for the particular year and the claims which have accrued up to 31 December 1983 in respect of the 1982 and 1983 calendar years.

(3) The premiums relate to risks which have been insured for 1982 or 1983. When an account is closed, certain claims are outstanding; either the amount of the claim cannot be agreed between the underwriter and the claimant or alternatively the

14

claimant is not in a position to finalise the amount of his claim. In such cases, an amount representing the anticipated claims which have not been settled is carried forward to the following year's account; thus, there is charged to the 1981 account and credited to the 1982 account the amount which it is anticipated may be necessary to cover claims relating to 1981 risks but not settled at 31 December 1983.

(4) Syndicate expenses are debited to both the 1982 and 1983 accounts. These cover such items as computerisation costs, printing, rent and office services and salaries, seats and substitutes, signing bureau charges, subscriptions and sundries. These are expenses directly incurred in running the particular syndicate and include the amounts payable to the underwriter and his staff and to the underwriting agent. The charge for seats and substitutes is the rent which is charged by the Council of Lloyd's for the 'boxes' which exist in the underwriting room and effectively form the underwriter's office. In addition to the underwriters, who are registered with Lloyd's, a further fee is paid for other members of the staff, called substitutes, who are allowed to assist in the underwriting. The signing bureau charges are costs incurred in recording the various insurances in a central organisation.

(5) The account for any particular year is credited with the interest, after deduction of tax, earned on the temporary investment of the funds of the syndicate (but not that arising on the deposit). The syndicate investments are revalued at the end of each calendar year. Any appreciation or depreciation in value over that at the beginning of the year or the cost of purchases during the year is recorded and credited or debited to the account for the particular year. In many cases, the syndicate investments are held throughout the calendar year. Monies received in an earlier year, which have not been utilised in the payment of claims, remain as investments until distributions are made to Members.

(6) The Member's personal expenses cover his Lloyd's subscription and amounts due to the underwriting agent. On joining, each Member agrees to pay an annual sum, representing a salary and profit commission, to the underwriting agent for his services in managing the syndicate's affairs. The annual salary will vary between £250 and £500 with the rate of commission varying between 17½% and 22½%.

(7) The deposit with Additional Securities Ltd represents deposits which have to be made in a number of countries before insurance can be underwritten. Additional Securities Ltd was

formed in 1937 to assist in financing deposits abroad. The company operates under two agreements, under which underwriters agree if and when called upon to do so to pay to the company an annual subscription equal to 25 per cent. of their premium income (other than marine underwriting) of the previous year. To meet local requirements in Illinois and Kentucky the deposits in those states are treated as being within the ownership of the underwriters.

(8) The closed account for 1981 would be included in the accounts but as the new underwriter would not be interested therein comments thereon will be made in Chapter 3.

2.8   These accounts give an indication as to the likely results at the end of the three-year period. The accounts made up to 31 December 1983 give little indication of the 1983 results but the 1982 account can be compared with the situation of the 1981 account at the end of 1982. For the purposes of taxation they are useless and need not be passed to the accountant dealing with the Name's affairs.

US tax return

2.9   Finally, the Name is likely to receive a questionnaire from American attorneys in connection with his 1983 income tax return. In this will be shown his name and initials and he will fill in his marital status, country of residence, and tax treaty country, the number of days he was physically present in the United States during the calendar year 1983 and whether he has any other source of income, apart from Lloyd's, in the United States. If he has any other sources of income, he must show the amounts of dividends, interest, salaries and fees in US dollars and also indicate the withholding tax suffered. If the Name owns property in the USA he has to give a description and the address of the property, the date it was purchased, the cost of purchase, cost of improvements, the dates occupied in the year by the Name, the dates let, the rent received and expenses attributable to renting the property. After signing the form he returns it to the underwriting agent.

2.10   A similar procedure is adopted during the second year in which he is a Lloyd's underwriter. It is only at the end of the third year that he is able to determine his profits for the first year for which he was an underwriter. It is at that time the major problems arise and the major decisions have to be taken. After the third year, the same procedure as outlined in the next chapter is adopted annually until the taxpayer ceases to be an underwriter.

3 The fourth and following years

Accounts

3.1 After the end of the third year, the underwriter receives from his underwriting agent a set of accounts incorporating the results of the first year of underwriting. These accounts are in similar form to those mentioned in the previous chapter but show the profit or loss for the year and the proportion due to the Name which is transferred to his personal account.

3.2 The account in **3.3** sets out for the benefit of each underwriter the total profit or loss arising on the particular account. The account includes premiums and claims notified by the Lloyd's policy signing office up to the end of the third year. There will be no further transactions in respect of that year. The administrative and clerical expenses for the last three years and appropriate to that syndicate are included.

3.3 The underwriter makes an estimate of:

(a) the unsettled claims;
(b) the claims which may arise in respect of the year being closed; and
(c) any continuing claims which might arise in respect of an earlier year and which were brought forward into that particular account.

The aggregate of (a), (b) and (c) are reinsured into the next year, i.e. the aggregate for the 1982 account is transferred into the 1983 account. Obviously, these estimates determine the profit or loss for the year. The auditors, the Council of Lloyd's and the Inland Revenue consider the basis of estimates. If the estimates are understated, losses are transferred to the year in which the claim is finalised. If overestimated the figures for the current year are unnecessarily depressed, and those when the claim is met incorrectly increased. As the Members of the syndicate vary

18

from year to year, excessive prudence or rashness affects individual Members. With inflation, each underwriter bears a heavy responsibility to make his estimates as near as possible to the final outcome.

3.3 The fourth and following years

1982 ACCOUNT CLOSED AT END OF THIRD YEAR

	£	1982 £	1981 account* £
Net premiums		8,496,320	
Reinsurance premium from 1981 account		5,431,710	
		13,928,030	
Net claims	7,125,275		
Reinsurance to close this account	5,950,921		
		13,076,196	
Gross underwriting profit		851,834	
Add: Profit on exchange		4,629	
		856,463	
Less: syndicate expenses		384,242	
Divided as below		£472,221	
Attributable to non-USA members (6080/6390)		449,312	
Add interest (net)		178,420	
Appreciation of investments (net)	£236,450		
Profit carried to personal accounts		£627,732	
Attributable to USA members (310/6390)		22,909	
Add interest (net)		3,211	
Appreciation of investments (net)	£27,140		
Profit carried to personal accounts		£26,120	

* In practice comparative figures incorporating the corresponding entries for 1981 would be included.

20

3.4 The amounts for interest and appreciation on investments are described as 'net'. The appreciation for a calendar year is computed by reference to the excess of the closing value over the opening value of investments held at those dates. This means it includes realised and unrealised gains. The appreciation is credited partly to the accounts for that calendar year and partly to the accounts of the two preceding years. The syndicate provides on investment income for basic rate income tax, either by direct deduction at source or by payment.

The Central Guarantee Fund requires payments to be made to it so as to provide a balance of monies in the ownership of the Society of Lloyd's to meet a general failure by any particular syndicate.

This is part of the policy of Lloyd's to maintain confidence in the institution.

A person may, if he so wishes, insure under a 'stop loss' policy. This means that if the losses exceed a particular figure defined in the policy the underwriter is repaid the excess losses thereby limiting his liability. The amount insured can be a fixed maximum amount or a sum determined by reference to the Name's loss after tax relief. The premium on the latter basis is lower.

Personal account

3.5 After the first personal accounts, which will not incorporate any brought forward figure, the personal account of the underwriter appears as follows:

PERSONAL ACCOUNT 31 DECEMBER 1986

Balance 1 January 1986		7,240
Less cash distributed		4,000
		3,240
Less Lloyd's Special Reserve fund transfers		2,412
		828
Less United States Federal income tax 1986	142	
basic rate income tax on investment income	145	
capital gains tax on foreign exchange profits	18	
capital gains tax on Lloyd's deposits	452	
		757
		71
Add taxed interest on personal balance	26	
appreciation on personal balance	721	
		747
		818
Add 1983 account net underwriting profits from summary of underwriting results		5,242
Balance at 31 December 1986		£6,060

3.6 Annually, the managing agent distributes to the underwriter the profits, subject to the retention of funds to meet transfers to Special Reserve Fund and, if the underwriter so wishes, to increase his personal balance. The leaving of funds with Lloyd's helps to create further capital for the Name. The income from the funds remaining with Lloyd's is brought into the computation of the transfer to Special Reserve Fund (see **5.7**) thus reducing the income tax thereon to basic rate tax. Gains arising on investments are charged to capital gains tax at 30 per cent. A major part of the appreciation of investments is not subject to capital gains tax because it consists of surpluses arising on the disposal of government securities held for more than 12 months or the disposal is after 1 July 1986.

3.7 The position regarding United States tax is complicated and is dealt with in Chapter 9.

3.8 For accounting purposes, United States and Canadian assets and liabilities are converted at the rates of exchange ruling at the end of the calendar year; for other currencies the conversion is at rates advised by the Lloyd's central accounting bureau.

Summary of underwriting results

3.9 In respect of the third year, the underwriter receives, in addition to the accounts described in Chapter 2, two further sheets. One sheet summarises the underwriting results so far as they apply to him and his personal expenses; the other shows his personal account. For each syndicate there is shown his share of the profit or loss and the various adjustments thereto. The summary of underwriting results appears in the following form:

3.9 *The fourth and following years*

SUMMARY OF UNDERWRITING RESULTS
1982 ACCOUNT

	Syndicate 10/250 Marine	Syndicate 10/251 Non-marine	Syndicate 10/252 Motor	Syndicate 10/253 Aviation
Share	60/6390	60/6204	20/5680	3/138
Profit	£5,894	£6,420	£465	
Loss				£170
Personal expenses	655	700	385	375
Profit before commission	5,239	5,720	80	
Loss before commission				545
Commission	917	1,001	14	
Profit after commission	4,322	4,719	66	
Share of appreciation of syndicate funds	2,220	2,946	760	196
Net profit	£6,542	£7,665	£826	
Net loss				£349

Total net profit
   transferred to personal account £14,684

Personal expenses:

(1) Agency salary	£300	£400	£250	£250
(2) Lloyd's subscription	150	150		
(3) Lloyd's Charities Trust		4		
(3) Lloyd's Benevolent Fund	6			
(4) Central Guarantee Fund	184	129	114	110
(5) Personal guarantee policy	15	17	21	15
Total	£655	£700	£385	£375

Notes

(1) As there is no profit in the aviation syndicate the underwriters are not entitled to a commission but continue to draw their salary. This is in accordance with the normal terms for underwriting agents.

(2) Every Member of Lloyd's has to pay a subscription to that body, to maintain its centralised functions.

(3) It is usual for underwriters to be asked to make annual donations by deeds of covenant to the Lloyd's Charities Trust and the Lloyd's Benevolent Fund and these amounts are usually paid direct by the underwriting agents and charged against the underwriting results.

3.10 As any reader will appreciate, the figures in the accounts show the results of the respective syndicates and the cash benefit to the underwriter. The figures do not represent the amounts on which tax will be assessed any more than in the case of the accounts of an ordinary businessman. Adjustments are made by the syndicate accountants to agree the taxable amounts. A Name cannot compute his tax liability or the transfer to Special Reserve Fund until he has received the necessary returns from the syndicate accountants.

Lloyd's taxation advice

3.11 It is usual for this information to be sent in the form of the Lloyd's taxation advice annually to the underwriter and/or his adviser in September. A typical taxation advice appears as follows:

FROM SYNDICATE ACCOUNTANTS

TO THE NAME

LLOYD'S TAXATION ADVICE
DATE 14 10 85
AGREED TAX ADJUSTED RESULTS 1982 ACCOUNT
FISCAL YEAR 1982/83

SYNDICATE RESULTS LOSSES denoted by 'L'			Syndicate No. 10/250	Syndicate No. 10/251	Syndicate No. 10/252	Syndicate No. 10/253
CASE 1 Profit/Loss			£ 3,021	£ 4,834	£ 48	£ 550L
Foreign tax included above, but available for double taxation relief, if applicable			84	39	21	—
Syndicate Investment Income	Gross taxed, per form LL 185E		2,500	1,420	398	170
	Net building society interest		—	—	—	—
Syndicate Capital Gains/Losses			2,333	3,508	958	244
	Exempt to Non-Residents	UK Domiciled	658			
		Non UK Domiciled	652			

Please refer to the notes overleaf.

REFERENCES

Syndicate Accountant	Member	Personal Accountant

26

The information, which is given in respect of each syndicate, is:

(a) the Case 1 result for the account which has been closed showing in respect of each syndicate the profit or loss together with a note of the foreign tax which is appropriate to that profit;

(b) the gross syndicate investment income for the year of assessment in which the account is closed, e.g. the 1982 account has related to it the gross syndicate investment income for 1982–83 (this income has been assessed at the basic rate);

(c) the syndicate capital gains or losses for any year of assessment covering the closed account, e.g. the 1982 account has related to it the gains of 1982–83.

3.12 On a separate form (LL185E (NEW) SYNDICATE) the gross investment income (taxed at the basic rate) and any investment income taxed at less than the basic rate. A typical form appears as follows:

LLOYD'S UNDERWRITER

Certificate of Member's share of gross taxed investment income received by Syndicates and/or underwriting agent (see Note (a))

I/We certify that the particulars given below concerning **UNDERWRITER'S NAME** of Lloyd's, London, E.C.3, for the year **1982** are correct. Information regarding the Syndicate(s) has been sent to H.M. Inspector of Taxes, LEEDS (UNDERWRITERS UNIT)

Signature   Date 14 10 85

Capacity in which signed: Syndicate Accountants   Address

INCOME   For running off year

For the Underwriting account 1982   (closed 1984)

Syndicate(s): (*see* Note (b)) 10/250	Gross amount of taxed income	income tax suffered thereon	Net amount credited to the member	Please do not write in the spaces below
				'I.R.' stamp
	£	£	£	
(1) Income taxed at the basic rate	2,388·00	811·92	1,576·08	
(2) Income taxed at less than the basic rate by reason of Double Taxation Relief (*see* Note (c))	112·00	20·16	75·84	
				'Duty assessed' stamp

NOTES

(a) Where income from the Premium Trust Fund, Trust Fund, Free Reserves and/or Special Reserves is included in the statement, the dividend vouchers have been retained by the Underwriting Agent.

(b) Insert Bureau Number(s) as in the list entitled 'Lloyd's Underwriting Syndicates'. If a Syndicate was differently designated for any year of account to which any of the above income has been apportioned, this should be specified.

(c) The difference between the gross income and the total of the second and third columns is the double taxation relief which has been allowed.

LL 185E (NEW)

28

3.13 The dividend vouchers relating to the syndicate investment income are retained by the underwriting agent.

3.14 For the purposes of the Special Reserve Fund transfer the figures for Case 1 profit and syndicate investment income are added to any interest which arose in the year of assessment on any personal reserves (see Chapter 5).

3.15 The foreign tax has been allowed as an expense in arriving at the profit or loss. If there is a profit, the foreign tax is added to the profit and allowed as a credit against the tax charged. If there is a loss, there is no adjustment. Any personal accountancy fees paid through the syndicate are disallowed but claims for such fees can be submitted by the Name to the Inspector of Taxes at Leeds (Underwriters Unit).

3.16 Similar information is sent to the Inspector of Taxes, who issues on Form LL9 a summary of the figures relating to the Name.

H.M. Inspector of Taxes
Leeds (Underwriters Unit)
Kingswood House
Richardswood Lane
PUDSEY
West Yorkshire LS28 6BN
Telephone: (0532) 562256

Underwriters Name

Address

Profits and losses adjusted for income tax purposes as set out below have been allowed as an expense in arriving at the profit or loss. Should the profit be effectively charged to United Kingdom tax a claim to double tax credit will be assumed and the foreign tax added to the profit and then allowed as a credit against the United Kingdom tax charged. Foreign tax is not shown where the overall result is a loss as double tax credit relief is not due. Syndicate investment income and any personal reserve interest itemised in the Syndicate accounts are also shown below.

Syndicate	Syndicate investment income	Foreign Tax (excl. US and Canadian)	PROFIT/LOSS (loss shown as minus)	Personal Reserve Interest Taxed at basic rate	Untaxed
250	2500	84	3021	0	0
251	1420	39	4834	67	0
252	398	21	48	0	0
253	170	–	−550	0	0
Totals	4488	144	7353	67	
Accountancy			440		

The above income for year 1984/85 will be reported to your main tax district but it must be shown on your 1985-86 tax return

LL9(Z)	Net profit	6913

3.17 The form shows for the closed underwriting account and in respect of each syndicate, the profit or loss, the investment income and foreign tax paid (other than tax in the United States and Canadian Federal income tax in relation to non-marine business in Canada). Where appropriate, it shows one figure for all syndicates in respect of accountancy, interest paid and the stop-loss etc. premium. In a cumulative column the net totals of Case 1 profit or loss, foreign tax and the total of the syndicate investment income are shown. This document is extremely important. It must be checked with the individual returns from the accountants for each of the syndicates. If correct, it forms the basis of calculation of the transfer to or from the Special Reserve Fund.

3.18 The amount of any stop-loss premium is deductible in computing the Case 1 profit (or added to increase the loss), both in computing the tax payable and the transfer to Special Reserve Fund (see **4.23** to **4.25**). Interest paid by a working Name to finance his Lloyd's deposit is allowed for tax purposes. The fee paid in respect of a bank guarantee for a working or non-working Name to cover the Lloyd's deposit is allowed, with the exception of the initial payment. Accountancy fees are deductible. Annually the amount deductible is agreed depending on the number of syndicates in which the Name is interested. The aggregate amount is shown on form LL9. The agreed amount must be paid for relief to be obtained. Foreign Names cannot obtain greater relief by reason of being overseas.

4 The tax treatment of underwriting profits and losses

Earned or investment income

4.1 Underwriting profits are assessed to tax under Case I of Schedule D as trading profits. In the case of most Names, however, the profits are treated as investment income and are, for years up to and including 1983/84, potentially liable to investment income surcharge. Section 530 of the Income and Corporation Taxes Act 1970 defines earned income to include any income charged to tax under Schedule D which is immediately derived by the individual from the carrying on or exercise by him of his trade, profession or vocation. In the case of a Name the trade is carried on not by him but by his agents. Where the Name is a working Name, however, underwriting profits are treated as earned income.

4.2 Broadly speaking, a working Name is a Name who is actively engaged in the business of Lloyd's and is employed full time either in the Room at Lloyd's or in the office of an underwriting agent or Lloyd's broker during the fiscal year concerned. In practice a Name is treated as being employed 'full time' if he spends at least 75 per cent of a normal working week engaged in the business of Lloyd's as above.

4.3 The distinction between working and non-working Names is less relevant now that the investment income surcharge on individuals has been abolished. It is however still relevant in deciding whether a Name is entitled to pay retirement annuity premiums in respect of his Lloyd's profits. Similarly in the case of a wife who is a Name it can be important in deciding whether the income can be separately assessed as wife's earnings.

Basis of assessment

4.4 Up to and including the 1971 account, the normal rules

Example **4.6**

governing the basis of assessment under Case I of Schedule D applied (i.e. the preceding year basis subject to special rules on commencement or cessation). The basis of assessment was changed for the 1973 and subsequent accounts and there were transitional rules for the 1972 account.

4.5 The current basis is laid down in paragraph 2 of Schedule 16 to the Finance Act 1973 and is very straightforward in that the assessment for any tax year is based on the profits of the underwriting account ending in that year, with no special rules for opening and closing years.

Example

A commenced underwriting 1 January 1980 and ceased on 31 December 1984. His profits are:

1980 account	£1,000
1981 account	10,000
1982 account	5,000
1983 account	7,000
1984 account	9,000

His assessments are as follows:

1979/80	Nil
1980/81	1,000
1981/82	10,000
1982/83	5,000
1983/84	7,000
1984/85	9,000

4.6 To effect the transition from the old basis to the new basis there were two Schedule D Case I assessments for 1972/73. The first assessment was based on the profits of account 1971 and the second assessment on the profits of account 1972. The result of this is that where a Name commenced underwriting on or before 1 January 1971 and ceases after 31 December 1972, whereas the profits of his first underwriting year will have been assessed $2\frac{1}{4}$ times under the old system, no profits will fall out of assessment on cessation as they would have done under the old system. To deal with this anomaly, there are special rules when a Name in this category ceases to underwrite. These rules are explained in detail in Chapter 8.

Underwriting losses

4.7 As underwriting losses are trading losses, the general provisions governing trading losses apply to them. They may, for example, be set off against general income under section 168 of the Income and Corporation Taxes Act 1970, carried forward against future profits of the same trade under section 171 of the Income and Corporation Taxes Act 1970, or relieved under terminal loss provisions in section 174 of the Income and Corporation Taxes Act 1970. They may also attract relief under section 30 of the Finance Act 1978 in respect of losses in the first four years of underwriting. Losses must, however, firstly be set against any special reserve fund withdrawal and secondly against underwriting income. A trading loss in an underwriting account is treated as a loss for the year of assessment in which the underwriting year ends. Thus, a loss for the 1982 account is treated as a loss for 1982–83.

4.8 Where relief is claimed against general income under section 168 the loss may be set against the income of the year in which the loss is sustained. Any balance which cannot be so relieved may be set against the total income of the preceding year provided the Name was underwriting in the preceding year. It will be noted that section 168 claims in respect of underwriting losses differ from those for other losses in that, in the non-underwriting case, losses which cannot be relieved against other income of the year of assessment in which the loss is sustained may be claimed against other income of the following year.

4.9 The order of set off is determined by section 168(4) of the Income and Corporation Taxes Act 1970 and the loss is set off against other income in the following order:

Working Names	*Other names*
(a) Own earned income	(a) Own investment income
(b) Own investment income	(b) Own earned income
(c) Spouse's earned income	(c) Spouse's investment income
(d) Spouse's investment income	(d) Spouse's earned income

4.10 A claim may be made under section 168(3) to restrict the relief to the Name's other income, i.e. he has the usual right of election to ignore his spouse's income.

4.11 The time limit for making the loss claim is two years from the end of the year of assessment in which the underwriting account giving rise to the loss is closed. For example, a loss claim for the 1982 Account closed 31 December 1984 must be made by 5 April 1987. (It should also be noted that where a Name has non-underwriting trading losses (e.g. he is a farmer) there is also a two-year extension of the normal time limit for making claims in respect of those losses.)

4.12 Because a Name, including a non-working Name, is carrying on a trade he is eligible for the relief available in section 30 of the Finance Act 1978 where he sustains a loss either in the year of assessment in which the trade is first carried on by him or in any of the next three years of assessment. Where a loss is incurred in the first four years of underwriting, the Name may elect to carry back the loss against the income of the three tax years preceding that in which the loss is incurred, taking the earlier year first. For example a Name who began underwriting in the 1979 Account and who incurs a loss on the 1981 account may claim that the loss should be carried back to 1979/80.

4.13 Relief under section 30 is granted in a similar way to relief under Section 168. In particular, the loss is set primarily against income of the same class and claims may be restricted to exclude spouse's income. For the Name there is once again a two-year extension to the normal requirement that claims must be made within two years after the end of the year of assessment in which the loss is sustained. In deciding whether to make a claim under section 30 or one under section 168 it is necessary to calculate not just the extent of the respective tax recoveries but also the respective repayment supplements and it should be noted that once a section 168 claim has been made there is no statutory right to withdraw it and substitute an alternative claim.

4.14 Where the losses are to be carried forward under section 171 of the Income and Corporation Taxes Act 1970 the normal rules apply. It is possible to bring investment income into the claim and the investment income which can be included under section 171(3) consists of:
(a) syndicate investment income;
(b) investment income arising on Lloyd's deposits, Special Reserve Fund and personal reserve Fund.

Terminal loss relief

4.15 Once again the normal rules apply and the application of these to Names is dealt with in Chapter 8.

Run-off losses

4.16   Where the accounts of a syndicate are allowed to run-off, the loss arising in any calendar year is treated as relating to the underwriting account which was closed at the end of that calendar year, e.g. a run-off loss arising in 1984 even if in respect of the 1981 Account will be treated as a loss of the 1982 Account (closing 31 December 1984). Where run-off losses continue after a Name has ceased underwriting see **8.7**.

Case I deductions

i Personal accountancy fees

4.17   The Revenue view is that no deduction is allowable for accountants' fees in respect of Special Reserve Fund computations and loss claims. Their view is that the only allowable items are 'fees relating to the agreement of the assessment to Income Tax or costs which can be shown to have been incurred in some way by the Name in earning his profits'.

4.18   The Revenue suggest guide lines in respect of personal accountancy fees which will be allowed as a deduction against the assessment on underwriting profits. For the 1982 Accounts the figures are:

First syndicate	£200
The next five syndicates	£80 per syndicate
The next ten syndicates	£30 per syndicate

These figures are inclusive of VAT. The maximum deduction for 1982/83 is therefore £900.

4.19   There may be exceptional cases where a greater deduction may be claimed, but the Revenue will require full details. The Revenue will normally grant the standard deduction automatically.

ii Annual subscription

4.20   This payment for Lloyd's membership, minimum £400, will normally be included in the reported Case I figures. Care should be exercised when dealing with new Names as often they meet the first annual subscription (with the entrance fee) personally.

iii Entrance fee

4.21 The entrance fee is not an allowable deduction for UK tax purposes.

iv Letters of credit and bank guarantees

4.22 The initial expense is *not* allowable unless it is to replace an existing deposit but the annual expense of maintaining these facilities is allowable.

v Stop-loss policies

4.23 Premiums payable under stop-loss policies are available for tax relief. It follows that any recovery under the policy will be brought into the Case I computation. The premium and recovery will be brought into the computation for the year to which they relate (except in the case of a continuing Name on a running off syndicate).

Example

	£
Reported Case I loss	4,000
Stop-loss premium	3,000
Total loss	7,000
Less recovery under policy	3,200
Net loss available for set off against other income	3,800

4.24 The amount recovered under the stop-loss policy will depend upon the terms of the policy. The recovery may, for example, be the amount of the overall underwriting result, or may exclude investment income and/or capital appreciation.

4.25 It follows that where there is Case I loss on *any* syndicate and there is a stop-loss policy in force, enquiries should be made of the Name to determine details of any recovery.

vi Interest paid

4.26 The tax allowance for interest paid was restricted by section 19 of the Finance Act 1974. Generally, interest paid by a

Name on a loan raised to finance an underwriting loss continues to be allowed for tax purposes as this is recognised to be a loan for business purposes.

4.27 The calculation of the qualifying amount is set out in the Lloyd's memorandum dated 27 March 1975. This is reproduced in Appendix 4.

4.28 Normally interest charged by the syndicate on a Name's unfunded loss will be deducted from his share of syndicate investment income unless exceptionally interest received by the syndicate is treated as part of the Case I income (in which case it will be treated as a Case I deduction in calculating the profit or loss for that syndicate). The interest is dealt with as being a deduction against the income of the account closing at the end of the calendar year in which the interest is paid, i.e. interest paid in 1984 will be allowed against the 1982 account income.

4.29 Where a Name borrows money to finance the net amount paid into his syndicate to meet underwriting losses or open year deficiencies (as stated in Appendix 4 at 3b) it is necessary to look at the combined results of all the syndicates and it must also be recognised that account must be taken of following years' profits. Again, the suggested method of calculation is set out in the Appendix and need not be repeated here.

4.30 It is interesting to note that if a Name pays interest on a debit balance with the syndicate, then that interest is allowed either against the syndicate investment income or the Case I figure without regard to the overall position. This may well be a profit which would give rise to no tax relief for interest paid. It is therefore sensible for a Name who needs to borrow anyway to do so from the syndicate.

4.31 Interest paid by a Working Name on a loan raised to finance his Lloyd's deposits will also be allowed for tax purposes. This relief is not available to Names who are not actively engaged in the business of Lloyd's.

5 Lloyd's Special Reserve Fund

Concept behind fund

5.1 The concept of a special reserve fund arose from an agreement between the Council of Lloyd's and the Inland Revenue when increasing rates of taxation prevented underwriters setting aside annually sums to meet future losses. To improve the stability of Lloyd's, underwriters must be allowed to set aside sums of money annually out of profits. Naturally, the Inland Revenue were anxious to avoid any question of the amounts set aside being exploited for tax avoidance purposes. The arrangements must comply with the requirements of the Tenth Schedule, Income and Corporation Taxes Act 1970 as amended by Schedule 16 of the Finance Act 1973. The investments representing the Special Reserve Fund must be vested in trustees who have control over them, have power to invest the amounts contributed and to vary investments. Separate Special Reserve Funds can be set up in respect of different parts of an underwriter's business. If all his syndicates are managed by the same agents, the underwriter has only one Special Reserve Fund but where he is in a number of syndicates managed by different agents there is a series of Special Reserve Funds. The income arising from investments of the underwriter's Special Reserve Fund must be held in trust for him, his personal representatives or assigns.

5.2 An underwriter is entitled to transfer annually to his Special Reserve Fund, a sum of which the gross equivalent is the lesser of £7,000 or 50 per cent of the profits. The maximum amount of the actual cash payment is £4,900, while the basic rate of income tax is 30 per cent. The computation of the transfer is set out in **5.7** *et seq.*

5.3 In determining the amount which may be transferred to Special Reserve Fund the profit includes:

(a) income arising from the investments forming part of the premium's trust fund of the underwriter, his Special Reserve

Fund or funds and any other fund required or authorised by the rules of Lloyd's or required by the underwriting agent through whom any part of the business is carried on to be kept in connection with the business; and

(b) all shares of the profits of the syndicates.

All charges related to those profits or the said income, being shares and charges payable to persons other than the underwriter and not otherwise taken into account, must be deducted. The amount which the underwriter decides to transfer to his Special Reserve Fund must be notified not later than 31 December following the end of the account. The payment must be made within 30 days of the date on which the Inspector has notified his agreement in writing to the amount of the transfer, or, if later, 30 days after the expiration of the 12-month period, i.e. by 31 January 1986. Because of the inevitable delays which must occur with the Inland Revenue having to process a large number of claims in a short period of time, as well as the similar problems in accounting offices, it is advisable to agree the amount transferable and make the transfer as early as possible.

5.4 Where an underwriter carries on his business during part only of the year of assessment, the maximum gross amount is reduced on a time basis. If, therefore, he is only carrying on business for nine months in the particular year of assessment, the figure of £7,000 is reduced to three-quarters of £7,000 or £5,250. As most syndicates permit people to resign only at the end of a year, this applies normally only on death. However many agreements between Names and underwriting managing agents provide for death to be 'deemed' to occur at the start or end of a year. Thus this apportionment is rarely made.

5.5 For tax payers whose investment income is liable at high marginal rates, the maximum payment should be made annually. The amount which is paid, grossed-up at basic rate of income tax for the particular year of assessment, is treated as a deduction from their total income for the purposes of higher and additional rate taxes, which includes the underwriting profits for the particular year and all investment income arising on investments held through Lloyd's. It should be borne in mind that when the balance of the fund is withdrawn on resignation from Lloyd's, the withdrawal is grossed-up and taxed as income of the final underwriting year (see **8.12**). For that reason, care must be taken if a Name is likely to retire in the near future.

5.6 Compared to the Annual Accounts shown in Chapter 2, in the fourth and later years of underwriting by the Name, a further sheet is added. This additional sheet shows the value of the reserves held by the managing agents in respect of the Lloyd's Special Reserve and any other funds.

Computation of transfer

5.7 The figures inserted in the calculation of the Special Reserve Fund transfer will be found from:

(a) Lloyd's taxation advice for each syndicate (see **3.11**) supplemented by the summary from the Inspector (form LL9, see **3.16**);

(b) the dividends and interests arising in the appropriate year of assessment on the personal funds of the Name (i.e. his Lloyd's deposit, earlier Special Reserve Fund transfers) and which will have been shown in his tax return for that year.

The computation is usually shown in a letter sent to the Inspector of Taxes (Underwriting Unit). It is inadvisable to send the letter to the Inspector in December and accordingly the majority of these letters must be sent in the months of October and November. A typical letter, using the figures in the forms in **3.11** and **3.16** shows:

5.8 *Lloyd's Special Reserve Fund*

Dear Sir,

[*Name of Underwriter*]

The transfer to the Special Reserve Fund for 1982 is computed as follows:

					Total
Syndicate No.	10/250	10/251	10/252	10/253	
Schedule D Case I Profit (Loss)	£3,021	£4,834	£48	£(550)	£7,353
Accountancy					440
					£6,913
Foreign tax	84	39	21	—	144
Syndicate investment income	2,500	1,420	398	170	4,488
1982–83 interest:					
Dividends					789
Tax credit thereon					337
Investment income, gross					1,160
					£13,831

35 per cent thereof £4,841; net 3,388.70
15 per cent thereof £2,075; net 1,452.50

Our client will be transferring the maximum amount to the Fund. May we have a note of your agreement please?

Yours faithfully,

Notes

The figures for interest, dividends and tax credit thereon are extracted from the tax return covering the 1982/83 income (i.e. the 1983/84 return) and represent the income arising on the personal reserve, Lloyd's deposit and Special Reserve Fund assets of the particular underwriter.

5.8 The basic fund transfer of 35 per cent and the additional fund transfer of 15 per cent must be distinguished. Where the balance of the basic fund is withdrawn on death there is no additional tax payable at the higher rates or at the additional rates. In the case of the additional fund, the nominal balance is related back to the year of transfer into the fund and tax at the higher and additional rates for those years levied on the grossed-up amount in the fund. There is no charge on the excess of the refunds over the nominal amount. This matter will be referred to in further detail in **8.9** to **8.11**.

Authorisation of transfer

5.9 Once the Inspector has received the Special Reserve Fund computation he produces form LL1(Z) which is sent on to the Managing Agent to enable the transfer to Special Reserve Fund to be made.

Inland Revenue
Income Tax

H.M. Inspector of Taxes
Leeds (Underwriters Unit)
Kingswood House
Richardshaw Lane, PUDSEY
West Yorkshire LS28 6BN

Your ref.

My ref.

Date

Lloyd's Special Reserve Fund

Mr.

Thank you for your letter of 28 Dec. 1985. I agree the basic proposed transfer of:

£4,841.00 (gross)   £3,388.70 (net)

and the additional proposed transfer of:

£2,075.00 (gross)   £1,452.50 (net)

under Schedule 10, ICTA 1970 for the year 1982/83. The balance(s) held in the Special Reserve Fund are currently:

35% £10,240.60   15% £4,388.82

This transfer must be made by 24 Feb. 1986.

N.B. Any dispute over the balance(s) in the Special Reserve Fund will not extend the period allowed for the proposed transfer under Paragraph 7(1)(a), Schedule 10, ICTA 1970 as amended by Paragraph 10, Schedule 16, FA 1973.

District Inspector

LL1(Z)

This shows:

(a) the balance in the reserve fund at 31 December distinguishing between the basic adjustment of 35 per cent and the additional fund of 15 per cent, and

(b) the amount to be transferred for the particular year at the respective rates.

5.10   On receipt of these details the managing agents charge the underwriter's personal account with the cost of the authorised securities purchased to cover the transfer. The securities constitute part of his Special Reserve Fund. The income on such securities is treated as profits from Lloyd's thereby enabling the taxpayer to set aside a proportion of that income to his Special Reserve Fund.

5.11   A similar procedure is adopted annually until the underwriter retires or dies.

Withdrawals

5.12   A Name may make an underwriting loss. If in any year of assessment a Name sustains an underwriting loss in excess of his Lloyd's investment income for the year, a withdrawal must be made from the Special Reserve Fund of an amount which, when grossed-up at the basic rate, is equal to the excess loss. In so far as the loss can be set off against the investment income, a repayment is due to the taxpayer, for on that income he has suffered deduction of tax at the basic rate. In so far as the loss has to be met out of the Special Reserve Fund the amount withdrawn is deemed to come first from the basic fund, i.e. the transfers which have been made with a limit of 35 per cent of the profits, and the balance is deemed to come from the additional fund. If the loss is greater than the investment income and the sums in the Special Reserve Fund, the whole amount in that fund must be withdrawn.

5.13   The amount to be withdrawn is calculated in a similar manner to the amount of any transfer. Assume that in the illustration in **5.7** there had been a Case 1 loss of £9,654. The amount to be withdrawn from the Special Reserve Fund is computed without any adjustment for foreign tax.

5.14 Lloyd's Special Reserve Fund

Syndicate No.	10/250	10/251	10/252	10/253	Total
Schedule D Case I Profit (Loss)	£3,021	£(7,214)	£(2,186)	£(3,275)	£(9,654)
Accountancy					440
					(10,094)
Foreign tax	84	39	21	—	—
Syndicate investment income	2,500	1,420	398	170	4,488
Dividends					789
Tax credit thereon					337
Investment income, gross					1,160
Loss					£(3,320)

Net withdrawal £2,324.00 primarily from the part of fund made up of transfers at 35 per cent.

5.14 The amount withdrawn is treated as income which has been received under deduction of tax. The Name sets off the Case 1 loss against the withdrawal, thereby recovering the basic rate of tax deemed to have been deducted. Any balance of the loss can be set against his other income in the order set out in **4.9**.

Case 1 loss for the year	£10,094
Special Reserve Fund withdrawal (grossed at the basic rate)	3,320
	6,774
Less syndicate investment income	4,488
Net loss available against other income	£2,286

5.15 The amount withdrawn is treated as taxed income. The Name can claim a refund of the tax deemed to have been suffered by setting off the Case 1 loss against the withdrawal. Any balance of the loss can be set off against the underwriter's other income.

5.16 Over the years, therefore, the amount of the Special Reserve Fund is increased by the annual transfers and decreased by any withdrawals; the latter being deemed to come first out of the transfers up to 35 per cent of the profits of the year. The amount standing in the Fund for tax purposes is arrived at arithmetically simply by adding up all the transfers in and deducting the nominal withdrawals. The balance for tax purposes may therefore bear no relation to the value of the investments in the Fund.

5.17 Where the working Name retires, his Special Reserve Fund up to that date is frozen. A separate Special Reserve Fund has to be set up for payments made after retirement. The calculation is made on the same basis as described in this chapter. For the purposes of identification, withdrawals to meet losses are deemed to come first out of the post-retirement fund and when extinguished out of the pre-retirement fund; in each case the basic fund is drawn in priority to the additional fund.

5.18 Where a taxpayer dies his estate cannot be wound up for a minimum period of three years. For each of those years, transfers cannot be made to Special Reserve Fund.

6 Capital gains

Syndicate gains

6.1 The Lloyd's taxation advice from the syndicate accountants shows the capital gains made on Syndicate investments, not those on the personal funds of the underwriter (which were covered in **2.3**). Any exemption due on government stocks is taken into account. Within the syndicate, the profit or loss on the sales of investments is apportioned to the three open underwriting years. For example, the profits arising in the year to 31 December 1984 will be allocated partly to the 1982 account (closed on 31 December 1984), partly to the 1983 account and partly to the 1984 account. Moreover, all stocks on hand at 31 December are valued at market value and any resulting appreciation or depreciation is credited or debited to the three open underwriting years of account in the same way as realised gains or losses. The syndicate capital gains assessed for any tax year are based on the amounts credited to the underwriting account ending in that tax year. This consists of a proportion of the gains, both realised and unrealised, arising in the calendar year to which the underwriting account relates and in the two following years. The computations will be agreed with the Inspector by the syndicate accountant, and the Inspector will then supply a summarised schedule (reference LL200Z) giving details of the capital gains on Lloyd's underwriting funds.

Inland Revenue

H.M. Inspector of Taxes
Leeds (Underwriters Unit)
Kingswood House
Richardshaw Lane
PUDSEY
West Yorkshire LS28 6BN

Telephone: (0532) 562256

Underwriter's name

Address

Lloyd's Underwriting Funds

Year 1982			Syndicate Gains	
Syndicate	Capital Gains	Capital Losses	NON-RESIDENTS ONLY Exempt Gains	
			UK-Domicile	Non-UK-Domicile (loss shown as minus)
250	2333		2333	2333
251	3508		2500	2500
252	958		720	715
253	244		72	80
Totals	7043	0	5625	5628

LL200(Z)

The form shows the total gains in respect of each of the syndicates of which the underwriter is a member for the year of assessment in which the particular underwriting year ends, e.g. if the underwriting year is 1982 the figures given are for 1982/83. The figures should be checked with the taxation advices received from the individual syndicate accountants. No additional capital gains tax is payable. The syndicate managers have accounted for the tax before crediting the net amount to the underwriter's personal account (see **3.5**).

Although the capital gains have been assessed on the syndicates, the amount assessed is apportioned among the Names and becomes a personal capital gain in the Name's hands which is dealt with like any other personal capital gain. For example, it may be covered by capital losses brought forward or, alternatively, it may attract a repayment because of the reliefs due to individuals for small gains. Equally, where the syndicate computations reveal a loss, that loss is not carried forward in the syndicate but is apportioned among the names and each Name's share is available to be used by him according to his individual circumstances.

The gains or losses which arise on the underwriter's personal reserves, Special Reserve Fund, Lloyd's basic deposit or Lloyd's Premium Income Deposit or Premium Trust Fund Deposit have been shown on the underwriter's personal tax return. He is responsible for paying the appropriate capital gains tax.

Review of liability

6.2 On receipt of form LL200(Z), the Name or his professional adviser must consider the overall capital gains tax position for the year. As individuals enjoy an annual exemption in respect of capital gains, tax payments on the disposal of syndicate investments may be excessive. If the taxpayer has not used his full exemption for the year against gains on his personal investments (including those relating to his Lloyd's deposit, Special Reserve Fund and Personal reserves) any unused balance will give rise to a repayment. The balance is set against the syndicate capital gains.

6.3 Should losses have arisen in the syndicate investments, loss relief may be claimed. The loss may be set against:

(a) the gains arising on syndicate investments in another Lloyd's

50

fund (i.e. where some syndicates are managed by another agent); or

(b) gains arising on personal transactions.

If there has been a net gain on syndicate investments in a Lloyd's fund and a loss on personal transactions, that loss can be set off against the gain.

Capital losses

6.4 Where the loss arises from syndicate investments and it is set against gains on personal transactions, the claim is made to the underwriter's main tax district. In other cases the claim is made to the Underwriters Unit at Leeds supplying the following information:

(a) the syndicate or fund in which the gain or loss arose;
(b) the reference number with the Underwriters Unit;
(c) the year for which the claim is made; and
(d) the amount of the loss on which relief is claimed.

6.5 In the case of those individuals who are not resident or ordinarily resident or not domiciled in the United Kingdom some adjustment may be necessary in respect of these capital gains tax assessments. This matter will be dealt with in Chapter 9.

Disposals within personal deposits

6.6 The investments contained in the Special Reserve Fund must remain in that fund at all times except where their release is authorised in order to meet losses. If the Name sells a security in the Special Reserve Fund the proceeds must be kept and reinvested within the fund. Any capital gains tax arising on the disposal is usually met out of the individual's personal account. A Name can apply for the release of cash or securities to meet the tax liability. If consent is given the sum released cannot exceed the tax demand. Where the transfer of the original security was made at a value in excess of cost to the Name, the withdrawal cannot exceed tax on the appreciation while in the fund.

6.7 Although the investments of the Special Reserve Fund and the Lloyd's deposit are held in trust by Lloyd's as security to meet any claims, the transfer of securities into the Fund and the withdrawals therefrom do not give rise to capital gains tax disposals. The normal rules relating to funds in trust do not apply. The Name is deemed to be absolutely entitled to the investments at all times. Where he has an investment in his own name and is anxious to make a transfer to the Special Reserve Fund, it may be advantageous to take an existing investment on which there is a substantial capital gain. The value at the date of transfer of that investment may be transferred into the Special Reserve Fund. There will be no capital gains tax payable on the transfer but it does enable the underwriter to satisfy the amount of the contribution. Subsequent to the transfer, dividends on these investments form part of his Lloyd's profits. The dividends increase the amount which may be transferred to the Fund.

6.8   Some syndicate managers are anxious that syndicate members build up the balance on their personal account. To do this they allow them to transfer investments held in their own name into the name of Lloyd's. This is an alternative to leaving part of the profits with the underwriting agent to build up additional reserves. Although no tax relief is obtained in respect of the transfer of these retained sums, the future investment income arising therefrom can be treated as profits in computing the amount of the Special Reserve Fund transfer.

6.9   Managing agents may invest the monies in the Special Reserve Fund in government securities. If these are held for over 12 months, any capital gain is free of tax but any loss is not an allowable loss for capital gains tax purposes. After 1 July 1986, Government securities are outside the scope of capital gains tax. The wealthy taxpayer, who would normally invest in low-yielding government securities, may while they are included in his Lloyd's deposit, Special Reserve Fund etc. purchase those with higher yields. Up to 50 per cent of such income may be transferred in later years to Special Reserve Fund unless the maximum profits of £7,000 have been achieved.

6.10   The usual provisions relating to the computation of capital gains by reference to the value at 6 April 1965 instead of cost and to pooling apply, except that an election for pooling all quoted securities does not apply to any in the underwriter's Premium Trust Fund, Premium Trust Fund deposit or Personal reserves. A separate election must be made for such securities. Each fund is regarded as a separate fund.

6.11 The ratio between syndicate capital gains and investment income is likely to change in future following the introduction of the accrued income scheme by the Finance Act 1985. It has in the past been possible for Lloyd's Syndicates to maximise capital gains by selling securities shortly before the ex-div date and thereby receive accrued income in a capital form. This will no longer be possible for disposals after 1 January 1986 as the accrued interest will in future be chargeable to tax under Case VI of Schedule D. There are in addition transitional forestalling provisions which can apply from 1 January 1985. It is not appropriate in this book to explain the operation of the accrued interest scheme in detail and for Lloyd's underwriters the calculations will be dealt with at syndicate level and notified to personal accountants.

7 Payment of tax

Income tax

7.1 The liability to pay and the date of payment of taxes on Lloyd's income depends upon the source of the income. The normal provision that the due date of payment cannot be earlier than 30 days after issue of the assessment always applies. All due dates listed below assume that assessments have been issued timeously. Income tax at the basic rate on the underwriting profits, which are chargeable under Schedule D, Case I, is payable one year and one day after the closure of the underwriting account giving rise to such income. Tax at the higher and additional rates is payable on 1 July following. If the account being closed is the 1982 account, the basic rate income tax liability cannot be calculated until the account is closed on 31 December 1984. The basic rate tax is payable on 1 January 1986; the higher rate (and prior to 1982–83, the additional rate) on 1 July 1986.

7.2 The basic rate income tax liability on syndicate investment income is deducted at source before receipt by the name. Either the managing agents invest in securities from which tax is deducted at source or they accept assessments on the basis that the syndicate is the taxpayer. The basic rate liability on the latter is due one year and one day after the closure of the account. The Name is not directly concerned, although he is responsible for the higher and additional rate taxes on his shares of the syndicate investment income. That tax is payable on 1 July following the date on which the basic rate tax is paid.

7.3 The tax on the capital gains arising from syndicate investments is payable one year and one day after the closure of the underwriting account in which the gains arise. The date is the same as for the Schedule D, Case I assessment. The tax is paid by the agent and deducted in crediting the appreciation in the value of investments to the Name's personal account. The due date of payment of capital gains tax arising on disposals, whether of investments in personal reserves or in the Special Reserve Fund

54

or in the Lloyd's deposit is the same as for any personal investments of the Name, i.e. 1 December following the year of assessment.

7.4 The investment income which arises from the Lloyd's deposit and any personal reserves, including income from investments in the Special Reserve Fund, is assessable on the individual underwriter in the same way as any other investment income received by him. Either basic rate tax has been deducted at source (or there is a tax credit thereon) or tax is payable on untaxed interest under Schedule D, Case III. Higher rate and additional rate taxes are payable by 1 December following the end of the year of assessment.

7.5 The foregoing dates are important in view of the interest provisions contained in section 86 of the Taxes Management Act 1970. Interest on assessments on underwriting income run from the normal due date; there is no two-year extension. Difficulties can arise in respect of assessments to higher and additional rate taxes issued shortly after the year of assessment. Usually the initial assessment covers dividends and interest received in respect of non-Lloyd's funds but it may also cover income from personal reserve funds. If so the tax assessment should be paid or a reasonable payment on account made to avoid interest charges. In so far as the assessment covers syndicate investment income it must be estimated. As will be clear from earlier chapters in the book, the figures are not available until the close of the underwriting account. It is not necessary to make a payment on account in respect of the tax on syndicate investment income since this is not due until 1 July, 18 months after the closure of the underwriting account.

7.6 The foregoing provisions apply equally to a working Name or non-working underwriter.

7.7 A working Name has to pay social security contributions on the amount of the Schedule D, Case I profit. For this purpose the Case I profits (adjusted for trading losses, capital allowances and any cessation relief) are taken into account before deducting personal reliefs, retirement annuity relief, non-business charges. The working Name's profits are treated as relevant earnings for the purpose of retirement annuity relief. A non-working Name cannot claim such relief because the income arising is investment income and not earned income.

Repayment supplements

7.8 Where income tax has been overpaid a repayment supplement may arise. Under the Taxes Management Act 1970, as amended, where a repayment of tax is made more than 12 months after the end of the year of assessment in which the tax is paid, the relevant time is the end of the year of assessment in which the tax is paid. For assessments under Schedule D, Case I at the basic rate, the due date is 12 months after the account on the profits of which the assessment is based is closed, i.e. for the 1982/83 assessment (based on the 1982 account, closed on 31 December 1984) the due date is 1 January 1986, while the relevant time for the repayment supplement is 5 April 1986. Prior to June 1978 under the then Revenue interpretation the repayment supplement would have started one year later.

Assessments

7.9 Shortly after agreeing and making the Special Reserve Fund transfer the Name receives an assessment in respect of the Case I profits and foreign tax arising from his various syndicates. The amount of the Case I profits shown in the taxation advice and form LL9 is after deducting foreign tax. Tax is levied, on the aggregate amount, without adjustment for the Special Reserve Fund transfer, at the basic rate. Any foreign tax paid is deducted from the tax payable.

Illustration

Using the figures in the illustration in **5.7**, the Case I assessment for 1982/83 is:

Underwriting profits	£6,913
Foreign tax	144
Amount chargeable to tax	£7,057
Tax at 30 per cent on £7,057	£2,117.10
Less foreign tax credit relief	144.00
	£1,973.10

Illustration **7.10**

It has been assumed the taxpayer's reliefs are covered by other income. No deduction is made for the Special Reserve transfer as this relieves tax at higher and additional rates only.

7.10 Subsequently, for the particular year of assessment, a higher and additional rate assessment is made on the Case I profits and the investment income arising to the syndicate. From the aggregate of these amounts is deducted the amount of the transfer to Special Reserve Fund. The balance is added to the underwriter's other income to determine the rates of tax. A working Name does not pay tax at additional rates. A person paying tax at only the basic rate does not suffer additional charge but a taxpayer with a substantial other income tends to pay as if the Lloyd's income is the highest part of his income. This situation arises because the assessments on other income have been settled before the figures of Lloyd's profits become available. Where high rates of tax are payable, say in 1982/83, at 75 per cent, a transfer of the maximum amount to Special Reserve Fund makes available to the taxpayer 45 per cent of the amount transferred. The amount available has to be invested and retained in that fund. The taxpayer is enabled to invest monies which would otherwise pass to the Revenue. But this relief enables a Name to provide additional reserves, which may be necessary to meet future Lloyd's losses. It gives effect to the intention expressed in **5.1**.

Illustration

Using the figures in the illustration in **5.7**, the higher and additional rate assessment are:

Underwriting profits		£7,057
Syndicate investment income		4,488
		11,545
Less Special Reserve Fund transfer		6,916
		£4,629
Tax chargeable at		
60 per cent	£2,777.40	
Additional rates	694.35	3,471.75
Less basic rate credit £4,629 at 30 per cent		1,388.70
Net tax payable, on or before		
1 December 1985 or 30 days after issue		£2,083.05

It has been assumed that all personal reliefs and lower rates of tax have been covered by other income.

Double tax relief

7.11 Once the taxes have been correctly computed and paid, the underwriter can relax until the next year when the foregoing is repeated. Double tax relief in respect of taxes other than US and Canadian taxes is calculated at Syndicate level and apportioned to the Name. The appropriate figures are included in the tax advice note and the appropriate claim is made by the Name's personal accountant.

7.12 Relief in respect of US tax is agreed between Lloyd's and the Inspector of Taxes. The Inspector will forward a copy of the calculation of the double tax relief claim that arises in respect of the underwriter's US tax. A typical computer report for a Name appears below, pp. 59–61 (the relevant figures are marked).

The Name need do nothing except claim repayment. The Name receives the amount of tax credit relief due by completing a repayment claim form and submitting it with form LL185 (NEW) SYNDICATE to the Inspector at Leeds (Underwriting Unit).

HM Inspector of Taxes
Leeds (Underwriters Unit)
Kingswood House
Richardshaw Lane
PUDSEY
W Yorks LS28 6BN

Tel: Leeds (0532) 562256 Ext:

District Inspector: C J Wannop

Your ref:

My ref:

Date:

Dear Sir(s)

I enclose a computer analysis of your client's 1984 US tax return which has enabled me to calculate double taxation relief as shown below. The individual amounts are shown boxed on the second page of the computer report. Explanatory notes are on the reverse of this form.

	Tax Credit Relief Repayable	Deduction
1. US underwriting profit related to 1981 Underwriting Account	**Nil**	
Deduction reduces profit/increases loss.		
2. US syndicate investment income A/C 1982.	59.70	
Deduction of the tax reduces the Lloyd's income for 1982/83, so releasing losses		
3. Capital Gains A/C 1982.	265.92	
Deductions allowable from 1982/83 gains, so releasing losses used.		
TAX CREDIT RELIEF DUE Total:	£325.62	

7.12 *Payment of tax*

Please forward a formal claim to the repayment now due, *together with Lloyd's vouchers (forms LL185) for 1982/83 to cover the investment tax credit relief repayable (item 2 above).* I will be in touch with you shortly about the adjustments to your client's liability resulting from the American tax allowable as a deduction from income/gains (if not already dealt with above).

Yours faithfully

C J Wannop
District Inspector
LEEDS (UNDERWRITERS UNIT)

NOTES

(All references to Regulations are to those contained in Statutory Instrument 896/1974).

(1) Tax on the American Underwriting profit for the Underwriting Account 1981.

(2) Tax on the American Syndicate Investment Income (both effectively connected and non-effectively connected) allocated from 1982, 1983 and 1984 to the 1982 Underwriting Account, assessed 1982/83 (FA 1973, Sch 16, (2)).

(3) Tax on the American gains (both effectively connected and non-effectively connected) allocated from 1982 1983 and 1984 to the 1982 Account.

For UK purposes the gains are assessable for 1982/83 (FA 1973, Sch 16, (6)). The tax allowable is restricted to 30%, the UK Capital Gains rate, where the US average rate is greater than this.

2—LDS 374245/1/E34094 40m 2/85 ELT

DOUBLE TAX RELIEF REPORT–U.S. TAX RETURN 1984

COUNTRY OF RESIDENCE UNITED KINGDOM

MEMBERSHIP NO. 10955K NAME
GRP/SYN.NOS. 10/250, 10/251, 10/252, 10/253

EFF. CONN. US TAX 850.00 TAXABLE I/C BEFORE EXEMPT 6484.33 U/W LOSS 81 CL 83 1058.67* US TAX 0.00 RATE % 0.00000
NOT ECON. US TAX 130.83 TAXABLE I/C 872.22 U/W ELEMENT 40.22 US TAX 6.03 NON-DTR I/C 126.74 US TAX 16.29

TAX RECONCILIATION SUMMARY EFFECTIVELY CONNECTED 850.00 NOT EFFECTIVELY CONNECTED 130.83 TOTAL 980.83
U/W PROFIT 0.00 INVESTMENT 0.00 CAPITAL GAINS 677.34 NON-DTR 16.29 NEC PERSONAL 124.80 TOTAL 980.83

INVESTMENT INCOME / INVESTMENT TAX

ACCOUNT YEAR	EFFECT. CONNECTED PURE NET	NOT-EFFECTIVELY CONNECTED DVIDENDS	NOT-EFFECTIVELY CONNECTED PURE NET	TOTAL	INV. TAX EFFECTIVELY CONNECTED	INV. TAX NOT EFFECT. CONNECTED	TOTAL
X	0.00	0.00	0.00	0.00	0.00	0.00	0.00
82	679.94	21.83	0.00	701.77	87.42	3.28	90.70
83	428.64	14.83	0.00	443.47	55.11	2.22	57.33
84	107.61	3.56	0.00	111.17	13.84	0.53	14.37
TOTAL	1216.19	40.22	0.00	1256.41	156.37	6.03	162.40

CAPITAL GAINS INCOME / CAPITAL GAINS TAX

ACCOUNT YEAR	EFF. CONN. ACCRUED	EFF. CONN. CAP. GAINS	NOT-EFF. CONN. ORD, GAINS	NOT EFFECT. CONN. ACCRUED	NOT EFFECT. CONN. ORD. GAINS	TOTAL	CG TAX EFFECTIVELY CONNECTED	CG TAX NOT EFFECT. CONNECTED	TOTAL
X	0.00	0.00	0.00	0.00	0.00	0.00	0.00	0.00	0.00
82	2873.23	50.80*	76.06	0.00	0.00	2949.29	379.20	0.00	379.20
83	1807.02	31.74*	43.93	0.00	0.00	1850.95	237.98	0.00	237.98
84	455.49	8.07*	12.41	0.00	0.00	467.90	60.16	0.00	60.16
TOTAL	5135.74	90.61*	132.40	0.00	0.00	5268.14	677.34	0.00	677.34

1977 ACCOUNT

RETURN YEAR	EXCHANGE RATE	INVESTMENTS INCOME $	INVESTMENTS INCOME £	INVESTMENTS TAX $	INVESTMENTS TAX £	CAPITAL GAINS INCOME $	CAPITAL GAINS INCOME £	CAPITAL GAINS TAX $	CAPITAL GAINS TAX £
82	2.35	61.69	26.25	13.46	5.73	447.32	190.35	100.72	42.86
83	2.02	392.59	194.35	1.26	0.62	2042.80	1011.29	0.00	0.00
84	1.70	701.77	412.81	90.70	53.35	2949.29	1734.88	379.20	223.06
X	1.70	0.00	0.00	0.00	0.00	0.00	0.00	0.00	0.00
TOTAL		1166.05	633.41	105.42	59.70†	5439.41	2936.52	479.92	265.92†

INVESTMENT TAX/INVESTMENT INCOME 9.11898%   CAPITAL GAINS TAX/CAPITAL GAINS INCOME 8.82302%

7.13   *The present method of calculating double tax relief for US and Canadian taxes is to change with effect from the 1983 Account.* A simplified method has been agreed with the Inland Revenue. Appendix 5 contains the literature circulated by Lloyd's on 30 August 1985. Relief will first be granted under the new system after 1 January 1987 when the tax in respect of the 1983 Account becomes payable.

The tax credit for the 1983 Account will be based on tax paid on the 1984 US Tax Return and the 1985 Canadian Return and the procedure will be:

(a)   Lloyd's will provide a report on the following lines (Appendix C of Lloyd's package).

(b)   This report will be sent to Leeds (Underwriters Unit) by June 1986 and a copy will be sent to the Name's agent for onward transmission to the personal accountant.

(c)   Leeds (Underwriters Unit) will not send a claim form but the personal accountant must claim relief by reference to the notified figures. It is suggested that claims should be submitted at the same time as those for relief for trading losses and repayment of capital gains tax.

It will not be mandatory for a Name to adopt these new arrangements but it is difficult to imagine that anyone will not do so because a Name opting out will have to provide for himself the breakdown of the US income and tax to the respective years since the Lloyd's system will not be able to calculate the apportionment. An election once made to opt out of the new arrangement will be irrevocable.

There will be some complications in the case of Names who begin or stop underwriting. For example the 1984 US tax should be applied to the 1983 Account but a Name starting on 1 January 1984 would not be involved in that account. In these circumstances, Leeds (Underwriters Unit) will hold the 1984 US tax until the 1985 tax has been reported and will apply both to the 1984 account. If full relief cannot be given the unrelieved portion will be carried forward for up to two years. There will be similar matching problems where a Name retires or dies and the principle will be that Leeds (Underwriters Unit) will apply the US and Canadian tax to the last two years of assessment and if still not fully relieved to the two before that. By this means it is expected that all tax will be relieved.

7.14   A further form to be completed annually is the US tax return. The underwriter receives the following type of form, partly completed with his name, initials, country of residence and tax treaty country completed.

UNITED STATES

INCOME

DECLARATION

1984

This declaration must be completed, signed and returned to
your Underwriting Agent by **15 February 1985.**

7.14 *Payment of tax*

1. United States Income Tax regulations provide different tax rates for married and single taxpayers. Therefore you should indicate whether you were married or single. If you were a widow or widower, or legally separated from your spouse under a Judicial Decree of Divorce or of Separate Maintenance as of the close of the calendar year, you are considered to be single for tax purposes for the entire year.
2. Income of spouse should not be included on this form.
3. The Country of Residence is the country whose income tax treaty (if any) with the United States will be applied in calculating the U.S. income tax due. If the preprinted country is incorrect, please so indicate by attaching an explanation to this form. Please enter the correct country if it is not preprinted.

4. If you were in the United States for more than 182 days during the calendar year, please attach a statement showing any capital gains or losses on United States investments realized in the United States during that year. The difference, expressed in U.S. dollars, between the cost and the proceeds of realization should be shown and, as the amount taxable depends on the period the investment was held, the dates of purchase and sale should also be stated. Capital gains or losses on investments sold outside the United States should not be included.
5. If you owned real estate in the U.S., please so indicate in Part II (2) and complete Part IV, which appears on the back of the form opposite. This Part IV must be completed irrespective of whether you received any income from the real estate to enable LeBoeuf, Lamb to ensure your continuing compliance with the disclosure requirements of the U.S. Foreign Investment in Real Property Tax Act ("FIRPTA").
6. Were you a partner in a U.S. Partnership or in a foreign partnership that did business in the U.S.? If yes, please so indicate in Part II (3) and attach a copy of the Form K-1 (1065) you received from the partnership providing details of *your share* of the partnership income and deduction items.

7.a. The income to be included on this form is that received during the calendar year from sources within the United States, other than from Lloyd's underwriting activities. Income is to be regarded as received during the year according to the date payment thereof is made in the United States. **Please show full details in PART III of the form and provide supporting vouchers.**

b. Each investment holding should be separately stated, and described so that it may be identified. Please state the number of shares held, the **gross** interest or dividend received from each investment, and the amount of U.S. tax withheld from each. **Proof of payment of withholding tax is required to claim credit for the tax withheld, and such proof should be submitted in the form of legible photocopies.**

c. Interest and dividends on the following classes of securities are not taxable in the United States, and should not be included.
   (i) Stocks, Bonds, Certificates or other Securities of a State, a Territory, or a possession of the United States or any political subdivision of any of the foregoing.
   (ii) Stocks, Bonds, Certificates or other Securities of the United States if issued prior to 1917 or where, under the respective Acts authorizing the issuance thereof, such investment is wholly exempt.
   (iii) Income from Eurodollar Bonds.

d. Income and capital gains from United States investments held as part of the Special Reserve Fund or Personal Reserve should be included subject to the provisions in note 4 above.
e. Any salary or remuneration for services performed as an employee within the United States should be shown under "Salaries", together with the United States tax deducted, if any. Please state the name and the place of residence of the person on whose behalf the services were performed. Director's fees and other fees from United States sources should be shown under "Fees". A deduction is allowed for expenses incurred in earning such fees. These expenses should be itemized on a separate statement. **Proof of payment of withholding tax as reflected on I.R.S. Form W-2 supplied to you by your employer must be submitted in the form of legible photocopies.**

8. **PLEASE SIGN AND DATE FORM WHERE INDICATED. RETURN IT TO YOUR AGENT BY 15th FEBRUARY.**

UNITED STATES FEDERAL INCOME TAX 1984

	TAX PAYER I.D. NUMBER	111-60-0200

PART I   To enable LeBoeuf, Lamb, Leiby & MacRae to file your 1984 Income Tax Return, please indicate if there are any changes in the information shown. Enter **only** the 1984 changes in the boxes below the shaded areas. if no information is shown in shaded areas, please enter 1984 data in appropriate **unshaded** areas.

	LAST NAME	INITIALS	MARITAL STATUS SEE NOTES 1 AND 2
DF001 **(16-20)**			
	(21-46)	(47-62)	(63)

	COUNTRY OF RESIDENCE FOR TAX PURPOSES SEE NOTE 3	AGENCY CODE	NAME CODE	LN CODE
DF002 **(16-20)**				
	(21-35)	(1-4)	(5-10)	(11-15)

PART II   **PLEASE ANSWER THE FOLLOWING:**

1. How many days (including vacation and non-work days) were you physically present in the United States during the calendar year 1984? SEE NOTE 4.   (51-53)

YES   NO

2. Did you own U.S. real property? SEE NOTE 5.
3. Were you a partner in a partnership that did business in the U.S.? SEE NOTE 6.

PART III   Did you have any U.S. source income other than your Lloyd's underwriting income during 1984?

YES   NO

IF YES, GIVE DETAILS BELOW. SEE NOTE 7.
The names of the payers of each item of income which you reported in 1983 are shown below. Please delete names of such payers which are not required for reporting 1984 income and add any additional names required for reporting 1984 income and attach schedule if insufficient space.   (54)   (54)

PROOF OF PAYMENT OF WITHHOLDING TAX MUST BE ATTACHED.
FORMS K-1 AND W-2 ALSO MUST BE ATTACHED WHERE APPLICABLE
(See Notes 6 and 7e)

(16-20) (21-22)	(23-52)	(53-60) **1984 INCOME** (U.S. DOLLARS)	(61-68) **1984 WITHHOLDING TAX SUFFERED** (U.S. DOLLARS)
	DIVIDENDS		
DF010 01			
DF010 02			
DF010 03			
DF010 04			
DF010 05			
DF010 06			
DF010 07			
DF010 08			
DF010 09			
DF010 10			
DF011			
	INTEREST		
DF020 01			
DF020 02			
DF020 03			
DF020 04			
DF020 05			
DF021			
	SALARIES—See Note 7e		
DF031			
	FEES		
DF040 01			
DF040 02			
DF041			
DF091			

SIGNED_____   DATE_____

7.14 *Payment of tax*

PART IV   Did you own any interest in real property located in the U.S. during 1984? This includes ownership of developed and undeveloped land, apartments, time-shares, vacation homes, interests in oil and gas wells, etc. If yes, please provide details below in resposne to those inquiries that are relevant to you. Whether or not you received any income from the real property, the information requested below is required by LeBoeuf, Lamb to ensure that you remain in compliance with the reporting requirements of the Foreign Investment in Real Property Tax Act ("FIRPTA").

1. Description and address of property:_____

_____

2. If the property is not owned entirely by you, what is your percentage interest? _____%
3. Number of days you or your family personally used the property in 1984 _____
   Number of days it was rented _____
4. Total amount of rent received during 1984 $_____
5. Annual Expenses Attributable to Renting the Property—**Not Personal Expenses**

	Amount
Advertising for rentals	$
Your related travel expenses	
Cleaning and maintenance (includes painting)	
Commissions, e.g. to real estate agents	
Insurance	
Interest on mortgage (not principal payments)	
Legal, accounting and other professional fees	
Repairs—plumbing, electrical, structural	
Taxes (property)	
Utilities	
Wages and Salaries	
Decorating (improvements less than $500—specify)	
Supplies	
Miscellaneous (specify)	

6. Date real property was purchased_____
      Cost $_____
         Amount of cost allocable to structure rather than to underlying realty, if known: $___

   Date real property was sold _____
      Sale price $_____

   Total cost of all major improvements (over $500 each) made by you since you purchased real property $_____
      Describe and itemize:

   _____
   _____
   _____

66

On the reverse of the form are questions relating to any real property in the United States owned by the Name together with spaces for any income or expenditure. In the form illustrated, the taxpayer's personal income, other than from Lloyd's, from United States sources is shown. He completes the relevant sections on the basis of amounts received in calendar years from the foregoing information and that provided by the Syndicate managing agents; the Name's US tax return is prepared and submitted by US agents. The Name or his UK adviser has nothing to do with this return. The figures are for illustration only. During the year, the Name will receive a copy of his US tax return and computer sheets. A full explanation of the form and computer sheets would require a treatise on taxation in the USA. On receipt of the return from the US agents it should be filed.

Canadian federal income tax

7.15 The Inspector will provide similar calculations to those in para **7.12** for Canadian federal income tax where the syndicate, of which the Name is a member, has investments or dealings in Canada.

7.16 Similar problems arise in connection with the amount on which additional and higher rate taxes are assessed on Lloyd's income. As it is the last income whose amount is known, the Revenue usually tax it at the highest rates applicable for the year of assessment. The underwriter or his accountant must maintain records of the position for each year of assessment on other income so that when the details of the assessments on the Lloyd's income are received, it is possible to check easily—

(a) the proportion which should be transferred to Special Reserve Fund; and

(b) the rates of tax which should be levied on the assessments.

The correct appeal and claim for postponement of tax can be made, without risk of unnecessary payments of interest.

Value Added Tax

7.17 Value Added Tax ('VAT') problems are dealt with by the managing agents. The individual Name is not involved. He is not required by reason of his underwriting at Lloyd's to complete VAT returns or to register with Customs and Excise.

8 Retirement and death

Cessation relief

8.1 As stated in **4.4**, the basis of assessment of underwriting profits changed from the 1972 account onwards and, to effect this transition, there were two Schedule D Case I assessments for 1972/73, one based on the profits of the 1971 account and one based on the profits of the 1972 account. As a result, where a Name commenced underwriting on or before 1 January 1971 and ceased after 31 December 1972, the profits of his first underwriting year will have been assessed $2\frac{1}{4}$ times under the old system, but under the new system no profits will fall out of assessment on cessation.

8.2 To deal with this, the Lloyd's Underwriters (Tax) Regulations 1974 provide that in these circumstances:

(a) The profit assessable for the penultimate year shall be reduced by an amount equal to the profits of the 1972 account. It is not, however, permitted to create a loss for the penultimate year in this way.

(b) The profits assessable for the final year will be calculated on an actual basis. Thus, if a Name in this category ceases to underwrite on 31 December 1984 his assessment for 1984/85 will be based not on the whole of the profits of account 1984 as would normally be the case, but only on the time based proportion from 6 April 1984 to 31 December 1984.

Example

B commenced underwriting on 1 January 1970 and ceased on 31 December 1984. The relevant Case I profits were as follows:

Example **8.3**

	£
·1970 Account	4,000
1971 Account	5,000
1972 Account	6,000
1983 Account	8,000
1984 Account	10,000

The assessments are:

1969/70 say ¼× 4,000		1,000
1970/71 first 12 months		4,000
1971/72 PY basis		4,000
1972/73 first assessment on PY basis		5,000
1972/73 second assessment on account year basis		6,000
1983/84 account year basis	8,000	
Less Cessation Relief	6,000	
		2,000
1984/85 say ¾× 10,000		7,500

If the profits of the 1983 Account had been only, say, £4,000 the cessation relief would have been restricted to £4,000 giving a nil assessment. There would not have been a loss created of £2,000.

8.3   Where the Name ceases to be an underwriter because of death, the assessment for the penultimate year is arrived at as in **8.2**. The assessment for the final year, however, will depend on the date of the Name's death and the extent of his participation in the account in which he dies.

Example

(a)   The Name dies on 30 September 1984 and participates in nine months of the 1984 account. In these circumstances his final year is 1984/85 and he is assessed on 6/9ths of the 1984 account.

(b)   The Name dies on 31 March 1984 and participates in three months of the 1984 account. His last year of assessment is now 1983/84 and he is assessed for that year on 9/12ths of the 1983 account, plus his full share of the 1984 account.

(c)   The Name dies on 31 March 1984 but participates in the 1984 account after the date of his death and after the end of the fiscal year 1983/84. Once again, his final year of assessment is 1983/84 because he cannot be assessed for a year in which he is not alive. The assessment will be on 9/12ths of the 1983 account, plus all his share of the 1984 account.

8.4 It is clearly of great importance to keep a permanent record of the Case I profit of the 1972 Account so that the appropriate relief can be claimed.

Basis of assessment on death

Underwriting profits

8.5 In **8.3** we have considered the basis of assessment on the death of a Name who commenced underwriting on or before 1 January 1971. On the death of a Name who commenced with the 1972 or later accounts, the position is slightly different. A Name who dies in any account will of necessity either die before 6 April or after 5 April. If he dies before, say, 6 April 1984 his final year will be 1983/84 and his assessment for that year is based not only on the profits of account 1983 but also on his share of the profit of the 1984 account. If, on the other hand, he dies after 5 April 1984 then his final year is 1984/85 and he will be assessed for that year on his share of the profit of the 1984 account (the assessment for 1983/84 will be on the profits of the 1983 account as usual).

Syndicate investment income and capital gains

Where a Name dies between 1 January and 5 April (and participates in that underwriting account) the syndicate investment income and syndicate capital gains of that account are to be added to the income and gains of the preceding account and taxed accordingly.

If he dies after 5 April then the assessments are on the account basis as usual.

Terminal losses

8.6 Where a Name ceases to underwrite and incurs a loss in the final 12 months of underwriting, he is entitled to terminal loss relief under section 174 of the Income and Corporation Taxes Act 1970. The loss of the final 12 months in so far as it has not been set against total income of the final year and the penultimate year may be set off against underwriting profits for the three years preceding the year in which the cessation occurs. For this purpose, there can be treated as if they were underwriting

Example **8.6**

profits, syndicate investment income and income arising from Lloyd's deposits, Special Reserve Fund and personal reserve funds.

Example

X resigns on 31 December 1984 after 10 years as an underwriter. His Lloyd's income has been:

	Case I	*Syndicate investment income etc.*
1984 Account	(16,000)	1,000
1983 Account	5,000	900
1982 Account	4,000	800
1981 Account	3,000	700

His other income is £500 per annum and his Case I profit for 1972 account was £2,000.

The terminal loss is £16,000 and this may be relieved as follows:

			Balance unused
			£
(a) Section 168 relief			
Total income 1984/85		1,500	14,500
(b) Section 168 relief			
Total income 1983/84			
Case I	5,000		
Less:			
Cessation relief	2,000	3,000	
Other income		1,400	
		4,400	10,100
(c) Terminal loss relief 1982/83			
Case I	4,000		
Lloyd's investment income	800		
	4,800		5,300
(d) Terminal loss relief 1981/82			
Case I	3,000		
Lloyd's investment income	700		
	3,700		1,600

The balance of loss of £1,600 is unrelieved.

Run-off losses

8.7 The treatment of run-off losses for the continuing Name was dealt with in **4.16**. It may happen that run-off losses continue to arise after a Name has ceased underwriting and in this case no losses can be allowed for any year subsequent to the year of cessation. Therefore, if losses arise in subsequent years they are related back to the final year. The Revenue have agreed that for this purpose the date of cessation is taken as the earliest of the following dates:

(a) the date of death of the Name;
(b) the date when the running off account is finally reinsured either by the Name individually or by the syndicate;
(c) the date when premiums cease to be receivable on long term contracts in respect of the running off account; or
(d) the date when all outstanding claims of the running off account are settled.

It is usual for outstanding claims on a deceased's shares in running off syndicates to be reinsured as soon as possible in order to obtain the release of the deceased's Lloyd's deposits and reserve funds.

Special Reserve Fund

8.8 A distinction has already been drawn between the basic and the additional transfers to the Special Reserve Fund and where the balance of the fund is released on the death of a Name, the distinction between these two elements is important. It will be remembered that where withdrawals from the fund are made while the Name is still underwriting, these withdrawals are deemed to come first from the basic fund and, only when that fund is exhausted, from the additional fund.

Withdrawal on death

8.9 The balance is released on the death of a Name after all the accounts in which he participated are closed. When the basic fund is withdrawn on death, it is not liable to higher rates of tax or to investment income surcharge. However, the nominal balance on the additional fund is related back to the year of transfer into the fund and the various elements are grossed up at the basic or standard rate for the year concerned. These grossed up amounts are then chargeable to higher rate tax and investment income surcharge, or to surtax as the case may be, for the year of transfer. For the purposes of identification, where part of the additional fund is withdrawn to meet a loss, the withdrawal is treated on a LIFO basis with the amount withdrawn coming out of the latest transfer which occurred before the year of loss, then out of the previous transfer and so on.

8.10   Where an assessment is made for an earlier year following the release of the additional fund on death, then any allowances, e.g. life assurance relief, which were restricted by reference to total income can be recomputed. Where the assessment relates to the year 1972/73, the transitional provisions dealt with in the Lloyd's Underwriters (Tax) (No. 2) Regulations 1974 must be applied. Briefly, under these Regulations, the tax payable for 1972/73 was found by first aggregating the 1971 profits with the taxpayer's other income for 1972/73 and secondly by aggregating the 1972 profits with the other income for 1972/73. There was deducted from the amount derived in the second computation, the tax on the other income for 1972/73. Thus, the tax on the other income for 1972/73 had a material effect on the tax liability on the Lloyd's profits for the calendar years 1971 and 1972. If there are withdrawals from Special Reserve Fund affecting those years, the tax liability thereon will be similarly affected.

8.11   It will be seen that it is important to keep a permanent record of Special Reserve Fund transfers and withdrawals.

Withdrawal on resignation

8.12   Where the balance of the fund is withdrawn on resignation, the amount of the nominal withdrawal is grossed up and treated as taxed investment income of the final underwriting year. In the case of a working Name, however, the withdrawal will be treated as earned income. The liability to tax which may arise on resignation may be substantial and the regulations do not provide for 'top-slicing' relief. The potential liability on resignation must be considered in making transfers to the Special Reserve Fund. It must certainly be borne closely in mind both in deciding on the timing of any resignation and also in any tax planning exercise for the final underwriting year.

Capital gains

8.13 When a Name ceases to be an underwriter, either as a result of resignation or death, he is deemed to dispose of his interest in the investments held by the syndicates in which he participated. There are no difficulties for retired Names because they will retire at the end of an account and, as the gains assessed each year in the syndicate include unrealised appreciation at the end of each calendar year, no adjustments are required.

8.14 The position is more complicated where a Name dies, because he will die part way through a year and, therefore, some of the assessments on the syndicate will represent gains or losses on investments held at his death, and on which exemption is due, since death is not a chargeable occasion. The calculation of this relief is complex and not the subject of this book. The calculations will be made by the syndicate accountants and notified to the Name's personal accountant whose responsibility it will be to claim any refund. Although the heading in Part IV of the Lloyd's Underwriters (Tax) Regulations 1974 refers to 'Relief from Capital Gains Tax on the death of a Member', the calculations can result in an additional liability arising.

Capital transfer tax (CTT)

8.15 A Lloyd's Name (whether he is a working Name or not) is carrying on a business and his estate is therefore entitled to the 50% business relief. This relief extends to the whole of his underwriting interest including the value of deposits and reserve funds. Moreover, the collateral backing any letter of credit or bank guarantee will also qualify for relief. The caveat should be sounded however that the Inland Revenue may question the admissibility of business relief on Lloyd's reserves if there were any question of their value being artificially inflated by outside personal investments which are not required for Lloyd's business limits. If this were the case the Revenue would seek to restrict the business relief.

8.16 Business relief is a very significant advantage and should be considered by the Name when he frames his Will. If the Name's circumstances are such that not all his assets will be bequeathed to his surviving spouse, it is sensible to arrange matters so that the Lloyd's interests are bequeathed other than to the spouse. This is because such assets, if left with the surviving spouse, will be exempt from CTT anyway on the death of the Name and, therefore, the business relief appropriate to the donor will have been lost.

8.17 A further result of the Name carrying on a business is that the CTT in respect of the underwriting interest may be paid by instalments over 10 years. If these are paid on the due dates, interest is not charged.

8.18 On the death of a Name there is a deemed transfer for capital transfer tax purposes of the value of his underwriting interest immediately before his death. Strictly, this interest has to be valued in accordance with section 38 of the Finance Act 1975, i.e. at the price which the interest might reasonably be expected to fetch if sold in the open market at that time. The Inland Revenue Affidavit should show an overall value for the whole of the underwriting interest with a breakdown of the figures between the deposits and reserves, any balance due to or from the estate in respect of a closed year, and estimates for open years. It will be readily appreciated however, that while the deposits, reserves and closed years may present no difficulties, it is a very difficult matter to say what is the open market value of a Name's interest in open years.

8.19 In practice, the personal representatives are allowed to elect within 12 months of the Grant of Representation either to value the interest on the estimated basis envisaged by section 38, or, so far as the value is attributable to open years, to value it by reference to the actual results of those years. If no election is made within the 12-month period, the valuation will be on the statutory basis. Whichever method is chosen the same basis of valuation must apply to all open years on all syndicates in which the deceased Name participated.

8.20 The valuation on the statutory basis is based on the audit figures which are produced annually for each syndicate and which provide a basis for an estimate of the likely profit or loss on the accounts for each of the open years. Normally, the accounts as at 31 December preceding the date of death are used for each of the open years, except in so far as the deceased's name participates in the account of the year in which he dies. If that is the case, then the accounts for that year are used. Formerly, the estimated results were adjusted to take account of the deceased's share of interest and appreciation. Thus, where the value was based on accounts prior to the death, interest and appreciation from 1 January to the date of death had to be brought in and, conversely, where the value was based on the accounts subsequent to the date of death, interest and appreciation arising after death had to be excluded. These adjustments are no longer made and this avoids the need for very lengthy calculation.

8.21 When an election is made to value by reference to the actual results of open years, then the actual profits received or losses incurred are taken into account. This method does have the attraction that it is easily understood and that CTT is payable on the actual sums received.

8.22 If the personal representatives do elect for the actual results and the Name's liability under any syndicate is taken over on the payment of a reinsurance premium, then that premium is allowed in full and treated as if it were a loss.

8.23 The whole question of the valuation of open years is a very difficult one and personal accountants acting for individual deceased Names will probably find it helpful to discuss this point with Lloyd's Panel Auditors.

8.24 Whichever method is chosen to value the open years, the result is aggregated with the value of deposits, reserves and closed years, and the resulting total is then discounted to arrive at the present value as at the date of death. The Capital Taxes Office published a memorandum on valuations for Capital Transfer Tax setting out their view of the appropriate discounts to be taken in valuing underwriting interests (see Appendix 6). Whichever method is chosen, the valuation of the underwriting interest is based on the results (either estimated or actual as the case may be) before the deduction of tax liabilities. Such liabilities, however, are of course allowed as a deduction for CTT purposes against the value of the estate as a whole.

8.25 The investments in the Special Reserve Fund (the value of which may of course be quite different from the nominal balance on the fund for tax purposes which is simply an arithmetical balance of transfers in and losses withdrawn) will form part of a deceased Name's estate for capital transfer tax purposes. A deduction will be given for any income tax or surtax payable as a result of a withdrawal on death.

8.26 The unlimited liability attaching to membership of Lloyd's passes to a Name's executors on his death and continues until all his underwriting accounts have been closed. This means that the possibility remains of further losses and that Lloyd's deposits cannot be released. A form of insurance, the Estate Protection Plan has therefore been devised so that Names can free their executors from some of the burdens of dealing with the estate of a deceased Name.

Membership of the Plan is arranged through the underwriting agent. The premiums payable are relatively modest and are deductible for income tax purposes. The advantages of the plan are:

(a) it automatically provides immediate and unlimited cover against any further losses after death on all open underwriting accounts and therefore enables the non-Lloyd's estate to be distributed without unreasonable delay;

(b) it enables the Lloyd's deposit to be released immediately;

(c) it releases the executors from their obligation to satisfy the means test;

(d) the estate continues to receive capital appreciation after the end of each account;

(e) the estate receives the overall net underwriting profit at the close of all the outstanding underwriting accounts but does not in the meantime have to meet any underwriting losses.

8.27 The estate of a deceased Name may contain assets liable to US Estate Tax. In the case of Name domiciled in the UK these are limited to:

(a) real property in the US;

(b) assets forming part of the business property of a permanent establishment in the US.

US dollar business derived from US sources is regarded as being derived from a permanent establishment in the US and this business is effectively connected with that establishment. The appropriate proportion of the Lloyd's American Trust Fund therefore represents assets liable to estate tax. For a Name dying in 1985 there is no liability where the US estate does not exceed $400,000 increasing in 1987 to $600,000.

9 Taxation of Names resident outside the United Kingdom

Introduction

9.1 For many years the number of non-UK resident Names has been increasing. These Names come from many different countries and the taxation in their country of residence of income from Lloyd's will depend on their domestic tax legislation and on the appropriate double tax agreement. In this chapter we will deal with:

(a) UK tax as it affects non-resident Names;
(b) overseas taxes in those countries which supply most Names to Lloyd's, i.e. United States of America, Canada, Australia, Ireland, New Zealand, South Africa and Guernsey.

9.2 A non-resident Name needs a tax adviser in the UK to:

(a) agree his UK tax liability;
(b) report on Lloyd's income to enable the Name to complete his domestic tax return;
(c) liaise with his local adviser on underwriting matters generally.

For example, it is of fundamental importance that a liaison be established with a US Name's agent. This is because ultimately the US Name's net of tax profit from Lloyd's depends not only on the UK tax paid but on the effect of the income and UK taxes in the US tax calculations. This comment may apply equally to Names resident in other countries.

9.3 All applicants to Lloyd's whether resident or domiciled in the UK or not may be admitted to membership on a means test of a minimum of £100,000. The rules governing categories of assets for means test purposes are the same as for UK Names and were set out in detail in **1.5**.

9.4 As with UK Names, non-resident Names are required to make a deposit with the Corporation of Lloyd's. Rather than transferring securities, the majority of non-resident Names provide letters of credit or bank guarantees mainly because:

(a)   they do not constitute an asset chargeable to UK CTT;
(b)   there will be no income or capital gains from the deposits or reserves to be taxed in the UK;
(c)   the Name controls the securities which form the collateral for the letter of credit, and
(d)   for US Names investments transferred to Lloyd's from US sources will attract a stock transfer tax unless a prior exemption is obtained from the Internal Revenue Service.

Letters of credit and bank guarantees must be in favour of, and held by, the Committee of Lloyd's and must be irrevocable subject at any time to a minimum of four years notice of cancellation.

United Kingdom taxation

Income tax

9.5   All members of Lloyd's are deemed to be trading through a permanent establishment situated in the UK. Non-resident Names are therefore liable to tax in the UK. There are special rules for US Names who elect for the 'special arrangement' but subject to that non-resident Names are chargeable to UK tax on all income connected with Lloyd's, i.e.—

(a)   worldwide underwriting profits (as reduced by any transfer to Special Reserve Fund);
(b)   worldwide syndicate investment income and income from investment in other Lloyd's Deposits (except interest on $3\frac{1}{2}\%$ of War Loan which is exempt for non-UK residents).

9.6   Relief can be claimed in the UK for:

(a)   personal accountancy fees;
(b)   the annual subscription to Lloyd's (but not the entrance fee);
(c)   the cost of maintaining a letter of credit or bank guarantee (but not the initial setting up costs);
(d)   premiums on stop loss policies;
(e)   overseas taxes attributable to Lloyd's income.

9.7   The basis of assessment and date of payment of tax is the same as for UK resident Names and has been dealt with in detail earlier. To summarise however this means that:

(a) The underwriting profits chargeable for any tax year are the profits of the underwriting account ending in that year. Tax at basic rate will be payable 12 months after the closing of the account. Tax at higher rates (less basic rate) and investment income surcharge (up to and including 1983/84) will be payable 18 months after the closing of the account. For example, the profits of the 1982 account will be assessed for the tax year 1982/83. Tax at basic rate is payable on 1 January 1986 and tax at higher rates and investment income surcharge on 1 July 1986.

(b) Syndicate investment income arising from the invested premiums will generally be received after deduction of basic rate tax. Tax at higher rates and investment income surcharge will be payable 18 months after the closing of the account. For example, tax on syndicate investment income of the 1982 account is payable on 1 July 1986.

(c) Income from Lloyd's deposits and reserves will normally be received after deduction of tax at basic rate. Tax at higher rates and investment income surcharge is payable on 1 December following the relevant year of assessment. Thus tax on income received in the year to 5 April 1985 is payable on 1 December 1985.

(d) Non-resident Names are liable for interest on late paid tax in the usual way but do not qualify for the tax free repayment supplement on tax which is overpaid.

9.8 Non-resident Names are eligible to make transfers to the Special Reserve Fund (dealt with in detail in Chapter 5). Transfers to and withdrawals from the SRF are based on income liable to UK tax and do not affect overseas tax other than indirectly by way of double tax relief. A transfer to the fund is treated as a deduction from UK profits in computing liability to higher rates of income tax and to investment income surcharge and a useful tax saving in the UK can result. However care does need to be taken in deciding whether a non-resident Name should make a transfer. It will usually be beneficial to make the transfer if the Name cannot get full relief in his country of residence for the UK tax paid. There is however no advantage if he can get full relief and in some countries it is possible to spread foreign tax credits over a number of years. Equally there is no advantage if he is liable only to basic rate tax in the UK. There could indeed be a disadvantage in that a substantial tax liability might arise on the withdrawal of the fund say on retirement from Lloyd's and moreover the assets in the fund may be liable to capital transfer tax.

In this area as in others it is necessary for there to be liaison between UK and overseas advisers.

Capital gains tax

9.9

(a) A non-resident Name is only liable to CGT on Lloyd's capital gains in so far as the assets concerned are 'situated in the UK'. This applies to Lloyd's deposits and personal reserve funds. As regards syndicate funds, those investments which form part of the Lloyd's American Trust Fund and Lloyd's Canadian Trust Fund are regarded as not situated in the UK. Investments held in the Lloyd's Sterling Trust Fund are generally situated in the UK, but any non-UK equities are regarded as situated outside the UK.

(b) A Name who is neither ordinarily resident nor domiciled in the UK is also exempt from CGT on gains from certain British Government Securities. Although no new stocks with this exemption have been issued since 18 March 1977, the following are still available:

$3\frac{1}{2}$% War Loan, 1952 or after	9% Treasury, 1994
$5\frac{1}{2}$% Treasury, 2008–12	9% Treasury, 1992–96
$5\frac{3}{4}$% Funding, 1987–91	$9\frac{1}{2}$% Treasury, 1999
6% Funding, 1993	$12\frac{1}{2}$% Treasury, 1993
$6\frac{1}{2}$% Funding, 1985–87	$12\frac{3}{4}$% Treasury, 1992
$6\frac{3}{4}$% Treasury, 1995–98	$12\frac{3}{4}$% Treasury, 1995
$7\frac{3}{4}$% Treasury, 1985–88	13% Treasury, 1990
$7\frac{3}{4}$% Treasury, 2012–15	$13\frac{1}{4}$% Exchequer, 1996
8% Treasury, 2002–6	$13\frac{1}{4}$% Treasury, 1997
$8\frac{1}{4}$% Treasury, 1987–90	$13\frac{3}{4}$% Treasury, 1993
$8\frac{1}{2}$% Treasury, 1984–86	$14\frac{1}{2}$% Treasury, 1994
$8\frac{3}{4}$% Treasury, 1997	$15\frac{1}{4}$% Treasury, 1996
9% Conversion, 2000	$15\frac{1}{2}$% Treasury, 1998

(c) As we have said earlier, syndicate capital gains for UK tax purposes are computed by reference to the appreciation in value, both realised and unrealised, of chargeable investments over the calendar year. That appreciation is credited partly to the account for that calendar year and partly to the accounts for the two preceding years. UK Tax is only paid after the account is closed.

(d) Where CGT has been paid by the syndicate, the syndicate accountant or underwriting agent will provide details of any gains which are exempt for the non-resident Name so that the tax can be recovered by the UK personal accountant.

Capital transfer tax (CTT)

9.10

(a) A non-resident Name who is not domiciled in the UK is liable to CTT on assets situated in the UK.

(b) A member of Lloyd's is regarded as carrying on a business in the UK. On his death, CTT is charged on the open market value of all his underwriting interest. That interest comprises his Lloyd's deposits, reserve funds and profits for open years. The valuation of the underwriting interest is covered in more detail in **8.24**.

(c) The UK tax authorities have accepted that as an underwriter is carrying on a business:

   (i) CTT in respect of the underwriting interest may be paid by instalments of 10 years, and

   (ii) a deduction of 50% of the value of the whole of the underwriting interest may be made under the business relief provisions.

(d) Certain government securities are specifically exempted for non-UK domiciled persons. The list is the same as those included at **9.9** above for capital gains tax.

(e) The use of letters of credit or bank guarantees will reduce exposure to CTT. This is because the Names avoid having investments in the Lloyd's deposit and thus in the UK. Letters of credit or bank guarantees cannot be used for Special Reserve Fund purposes.

(g) In any event provided a non-UK domiciled Name has no other assets situated in the UK under present rates of tax no CTT will be payable until the value of his underwriting interest exceeds £134,000. This is because of the 50% business relief which will reduce the value to £67,000 which is the limit of the nil rate band.

Relief for US and Canadian tax

9.11   Many syndicates have significant amounts of business in the United States and Canada. Each Name has to pay US and Canadian tax on his share of underwriting profits and investment income arising in those countries. A Name who is not resident in the UK is not entitled to double taxation relief in respect of this tax but he may offset it against the gross income chargeable to UK tax.

Taxation in other countries

9.12 The following sections provide an outline of the tax consequences in the respective countries of a citizen of that country becoming a Name at Lloyd's.

United States of America

9.13 *General*

Lloyd's underwriters including US Names are subject to the terms of a Closing Agreement with the US Internal Revenue Service. It is important that its terms be complied with in the interests of all members of Lloyd's.

The following notes which include the requirements of the Closing Agreement are intended as a general guide only. They relate to US Federal tax, but there are also state and city taxes. Liaison with the US agent is important for detailed information.

Underwriting income and gains

(a) A US citizen or resident is liable to US Federal tax on his worldwide income, but receives foreign tax credit in respect of UK tax paid on his Lloyd's income (subject to the credit limit rules).

(b) For the majority of Names the US tax year runs to 31 December. Under the Closing Agreement syndicate investment income and gains are chargeable in the US in the year in which they arise, irrespective of the underwriting account to which they are credited. Underwriting profits are chargeable in the year in which they are distributed.

(c) In the US capital gains are taxed as income, but there is a distinction between short term and long term gains. Short term gains are those arising on disposals within 6 months or less of purchase and are taxed in full. Currently only 40% of long term gains are chargeable. Any accrued interest included in the purchase or selling price of fixed interest securities is generally treated as interest for US tax purposes.

(d) A new Name will receive no income from Lloyd's until the conclusion of his third year and will suffer US tax on investment income and gains before he actually receives them.

This is so even if the US Name is taxable on a cash basis on his other US income.

(e) For example, if a Name commenced on 1 January 1984, he will receive nothing until 1987, when the profits of the 1984 Underwriting Account are distributed. Nevertheless, tax will be payable in the US on the following:

> Calendar Year 1984 – Name's share of 1984 investment income and gains allocated to 1984 Underwriting Account.
>
> Calendar Year 1985 – Name's share of 1985 investment income and gains allocated to 1984 and 1985 Underwriting Accounts.
>
> Calendar Year 1986 – Name's share of 1986 investment income and gains allocated to 1984, 1985 and 1986 Underwriting Accounts.
>
> Calendar Year 1987 – Profits of 1984 Underwriting Account plus Name's share of 1987 investment income and gains.

(f) US Names who incur losses may offset these against their other income. Normally losses which cannot be used in the year of loss are (within limits) available to carry back or forward.

Deductible expenses

(a) The annual subscription is allowable for US tax but there is some uncertainty about the entrance fee. Some Names have been successful in claiming a deduction in the year of payment whereas others have had to amortise the fee and claim it over a number of years.

(b) A Member's annual travelling expenses to the UK for the purpose of visiting Lloyd's are allowed in the US but if there is a dual purpose to the visit, then the costs must be apportioned.

(c) All other expenses that are allowed for UK tax are also allowed for US tax. These will include personal accountants fees, stop loss premiums, letters of credit or bank guarantee charges.

Special Reserve Fund

Transfers to and from the SRE may have no consequence as far as the calculation of the US tax liability is concerned. They do, however, affect UK tax and, therefore, the amount of double tax relief in the US so that in some circumstances use of the SRF can be attractive for US Names.

Exchange gains and losses

The reported figures for US returns (see below) will have been calculated mainly from the syndicate accounts. There will inevitably be a different exchange rate at the time when sums are paid by the syndicate to the Name. It is understood that a US Name may include the resultant gains or losses but must do so consistently year by year.

Foreign taxes

The aim must be to ensure that credit is allowed for UK tax to the full extent allowable under US law, and that credits are not lost through failure to match tax payments with income.

(a) US taxpayers receive relief from double taxation of foreign source income through a credit against US tax liability for foreign income taxes paid or accrued. However, the credit is subject to various limitations. For example, the credit may not exceed the proportion of the US tax which the taxpayer's income from sources outside the US bears to his entire adjusted taxable income.

(b) It is necessary to know whether a US Name has elected for the cash or accrual method for his foreign tax credit. Most elect for the cash method. For them it will often be advantageous to make cash payments of UK tax within the year in which the related income is reportable for US tax purposes. For example, 1983 Underwriting Account profits would normally be reported by a US Name in his 1986 US tax return. The UK tax payable in respect of such income would be due 1 January 1987. By prepaying the UK tax before the end of 1986, the US Name would be enabled to claim foreign tax credit for the UK tax in his 1986 US return, instead of having to wait a year for the credit. He would also be less likely to run into limitations on the credit allowable, since the income and tax would fall in the same year's return.

(c) Because of the 'tax shelter' rules within the US tax system it often happens that although the Lloyd's income may form only a relatively small part of the Names actual total worldwide income, it can represent a substantial proportion of the

US taxable income. In such circumstances it can often be difficult to obtain full double tax relief for UK tax because of the 'proportion' rule mentioned in (a) above and early liaison with the US agent is clearly very necessary.

Surplus credits may be minimised by:

(i)   use of payments into the Special Reserve Fund which defer the UK tax liability;

(i)   creating foreign source income with low amounts of foreign tax;

(iii) timing payments of UK tax so that the effect of the 'proportion' rule does not create substantial surplus credits.

US returns

(a) A US Name with a taxable year ending on 31 December 1984 must file a return with the Internal Revenue Service by 15 April 1985 showing details of the investment income and gains for 1984 and the underwriting profit of the 1981 account released in 1984. At the same time, the Name must file an estimate of the investment income and gains for 1985 and an estimate of the 1982 underwriting profits. Tax is paid quarterly on the 1985 estimates, any balance being made good when the return of actual income is filed on 15 April 1986.

(b) It is possible to obtain an extension of time or to correct a return previously made.

(c) There are penalties if a return is filed late without a prior extension of time being granted or if it is filed outside the extended period. Penalties may also be imposed if the estimated tax payments fall materially below the final tax due.

(d) Any US citizens not resident in the US must still file annual returns. They may exclude certain income from their return but it is understood that Lloyd's income must be included. They may still claim tax credit for the UK taxes paid on Lloyd's income.

(e) A special advice will be issued in March each year by the syndicate accountants or underwriting agent to enable the Name to file details in his US return.

(f) The figure reported for US purposes will not compare with those in the Name's personal account supplied by his underwriting agent as:

(i)   The personal account shows investment income and gains credited to an Underwriting Account whereas the US figures reported show the income and gains arising in a calendar year (which are apportioned to three Underwriting Accounts);

(ii) in the UK capital gains tax is chargeable on both realised and unrealised syndicate gains (and this is the amount which after providing for tax is shown as capital appreciation in the Name's personal account) whereas only realised gains are reported for US purposes; and

(iii) accrued interest on purchases and sales of investment is treated as capital for UK tax prior to 1 January 1986, whereas normally this is income for US tax.

(g) For 1984 it will be necessary to report capital gains separately for the periods 1 January to 22 June 1984 and 23 June 1984 to 31 December 1984. This is due to provisions in the US 1984 Tax Act.

Reporting

(a) The personal accountant in the UK will report as instructed by the US Name but will normally be required to:
  (i) give advice concerning taxation and other implications of underwriting membership of Lloyd's;
  (ii) report the total income from all syndicate and personal funds in the necessary form to the Name's US taxation advisers in good time for the return to be submitted to the Internal Revenue Service by the 15 April; and
  (iii) prepare the UK tax return and agree all UK tax liabilities and residence status.

It is recognised as vital that the information provided for the US return is as accurate as possible and is provided in good time.

(b) Details of syndicate investment income and gains and trading profits are obtained from the syndicate accountants or underwriting agents and will be computed by them in accordance with US tax principles. Any other UK income and gains must also be included in the report made by the UK personal accountant, e.g. any income from Lloyd's deposits. Such income must again be reported in accordance with US tax principles. Many Names will have no other such income (where for example they are using a letter of credit).

(c) A report in a form approved by Lloyd's will be provided by the UK personal accountant. This provides for the separate reporting of interest on certain bonds which are exempt from federal tax and possibly state or city taxes. These exemptions depend either on the type of investment or the Name's state or city of residence.

The special arrangement for UK tax

There is a 'special arrangement' for Names who are resident in the US giving relief calculated by reference to the Lloyd's income regarded as attributable to business carried on in the US. This arrangement is not available to US citizens resident outside the US. For a new Name the election for the special arrangement should be deferred until it is clear there is some relief due. If, for example, there is a loss on US source business the election will result in more tax being payable in the UK. Full details are contained in a Lloyd's summary but the main points are as set out below.

(a) The Name must elect for the special treatment and the effect is that he is then exempt from UK tax on:
  (i) that part of his underwriting profits which represent US source income, which is defined as profit deriving from:
    (aa) direct and reinsurance business placed through a US broker; and
    (bb) direct insurance of US situs risks not placed through a US broker.
  (ii) syndicate investment income arising from the investment of premiums related to US source business;
  (iii) the proportion of income from Lloyd's deposits and reserves which US premium income bears to total premium income, (subject to an overriding provision limiting relief to US source investment income).

(b) A Name who has made the election will therefore be liable to UK tax on the following sources of income:
  (i) underwriting profits on non US business;
  (ii) syndicate income arising from the invested premiums not related to US source business; and
  (iii) income from Lloyd's deposits and reserves (which will normally be received under deduction of tax)

(c) The formal election for the special arrangement must be made by the Name within three years of the end of the first fiscal year for which it is to have effect. For example, an election to take the relief with effect from the 1982 Underwriting Account must be made by 5 April 1986. The election remains in force until revoked (there is a similar three year time limit for revocation), but once revoked cannot subsequently be renewed.

(d) Where an election is made, no relief can be obtained against other UK income for underwriting losses sustained on US source business.

(e) Once an election has been made:
  (i) Lloyd's issues special forms each year to the Name's personal accountant in the UK, who enter details of any income from special and personal reserves and Lloyd's deposits;
  (ii) the syndicate accountants or underwriting agents will enter the syndicate investment income, income and gains effectively connected with the US;
  (iii) the completed forms are then forwarded by the personal accountant to Lloyd's. The Inland Revenue will advise the personal accountant of the agreed amount of exemption; and
  (iv) following the agreement of the US source income an income tax assessment will be made on the underwriting trading profits after excluding the US effectively connected element.

(h) In the UK income tax at basic rate on investment income is deducted at source (through the syndicate). A credit should be claimed in respect of that part effectively connected with the US.

Estate duty/capital transfer tax

The US has a unified system of estate and gift taxation. Various states may impose separate estate and gift taxes although these are creditable (within limitations) against the federal estate tax.

To avoid international double taxation the statutory rules have been modified by a treaty in force with the UK.

UK capital transfer tax can be minimised by the use of letters of credit or bank guarantees and limiting investments to those specifically exempted.

Exchange control

The US has no exchange controls.

Canada

9.14 *General*

A Canadian resident is taxable on his worldwide income. The Canadian taxation authorities (Revenue Canada) have accepted the general UK taxation principles of assessing Lloyd's income by reference to underwriting accounts. The income is assessable on a 'receipts' basis. For example the profits of the 1982 underwriting account (closed 31 December 1984) distributed to Names during 1985 will be included in the Candian Name's 1985 Canadian tax return.

Canada does however insist on some changes in the way the income and gains of an underwriting account are calculated for Canadian tax purposes.

Underwriting income and capital gains

The main difference from UK tax treatments prior to 1 January 1986 is that for syndicate investments, accrued interest bought and sold with a fixed interest security is generally treated as income, not as a capital gain. There is no separate capital gains tax but 50% of any capital gain (which is called 'taxable capital gain') is treated as income for Canadian tax purposes. For this purpose, taxable capital gains include 50% of all gains (realised and unrealised) allocated to the underwriting account regardless of the fact that some of these gains are exempt from UK tax for one reason or another.

If underwriting losses less investment income from syndicate funds and investment income from Lloyd's deposits and personal reserves aggregate to a loss in a year, then the loss can be set against the following items in the order shown:

- other income earned in the year
- taxable capital gains of the year
- net income earned in the preceding three years
- net income earned in the subsequent seven years

Capital gains and losses generated in personal reserve funds are only recognised in the year they are realised.

Capital losses can be set off against capital gains and other income according to the provisions of the Canadian Income Tax Act.

Deductible expenses

(a) The entrance fee and associated legal costs paid on admission to Lloyd's membership are 'eligible capital expenditures' of the year of payment. One half may be set off against Canadian tax by amortisation at a rate of 10% on a diminishing balance basis.

(b) Letter of credit/bank guarantee costs are deductible.

(c) Stop loss premiums and estate protection plan premiums are allowed against the profit of the year of underwriting account to which the premium related.

(d) UK and Canadian accounting fees are deductible.

(e) Travel costs to Lloyd's are deductible.

These deductions are normally not available in the year of payment but against income of the account when reported.

Special reserve fund

Transfers to and from the SRF have no impact on the Canadian tax calculation other than indirectly through the effect on the amount of foreign tax credit available.

Foreign taxes

Revenue Canada allows foreign taxes as a credit. The amount of foreign tax allowable, however, will be reduced by the proportion of Lloyd's income that has a Canadian source.

Further, the foreign tax credit is restricted by an effective rate limitation.

Exchange gains/losses

Revenue Canada require all Lloyd's income, gains, expenses and foreign taxes to be converted from sterling to Canadian currency at the average exchange rate of the calendar year in which the account profits are remitted to the Name (which is the year after the year the account closes).

Canadian returns

The UK personal accountant will provide Canadian resident Names with a taxation advice calculated on the Canadian tax basis. In addition to detailing the income, gains, expenses and foreign taxes of the relevant underwriting account, the advice will also indicate the proportion of the profit that is regarded as being effectively connected with (i.e. arising in) Canada.

An example of the type of report is shown below.

The return of Lloyd's income and gains must be made by 30 April following the year in which an underwriting account's results have been distributed.

Estate duty

Canada has no federal or provincial inheritance duties (except for Quebec). There is therefore no possibility of any credit for UK capital transfer tax paid. Care should be taken to minimise such liability by the use of Letters of Credit or bank guarantees and by limiting investments to those specifically exempted from CTT.

Exchange control

Canada has no monetary exchange controls of any kind.

CANADIAN ADVICE NOTICE

Dear Sir,

1984 CANADIAN TAX RETURN
1981 LLOYD'S UNDERWRITING ACCOUNT

We set out below the information required for inclusion in the Canadian Tax Return for the year 1984. The figures are the totals for all syndicates for the 1981 account and are computed as required for Canadian tax purposes.

1   1981 ACCOUNT INCOME

1.1	Underwriting profit/(loss)	£
1.2	Investment income from syndicate funds	
1.3	Capital gain/(loss) on syndicate funds – 50%	
		£

2   EXPENSES INCURRED IN EARNING INCOME
    (not already deducted in arriving at figures 1 above)

2.1	UK Accounting fees	£
2.2	Letter of Credit or bank guarantee charges	
2.3	Stop loss premium	
2.4	Other	
		£

The amounts shown above do not include additional expenses incurred personally.

3 FOREIGN TAXES

3.1	Withheld at source – 1981 Account	£
3.2	Paid in 1984 (normally 1980 account taxes)	
		£

4 CANADIAN SHARE OF PREMIUM INCOME

4.1 Canadian premium income
4.2 World wide premium income

Relevant percentage _____ %

No acknowledgement of this advice is necessary.

Australia

9.15 *General*

If a person is resident in Australia most of the income he derives is subject to income tax in Australia. However, income arising outside Australia (other than dividends) which has suffered income tax in the country of origin is exempt under the provisions of section 23(q) of the Australian Income Tax Act.

Underwriting income and gains

Income   Most Lloyd's income being subject to income tax in the UK or elsewhere is exempt from tax in Australia. This will include underwriting profits and interest arising on deposits forming part of the Lloyd's deposit, special or personal reserve funds and any capital profits taxed as income, e.g. in the United States.

The section 23(q) exemption does not apply to:
(a) interest on $3\frac{1}{2}$% War Loan which is exempt (for non resident names) from UK tax; and
(b) dividends.

Australian income tax liability will arise on these items.

Gains   There is no capital gains tax in Australia, but the profit on the sale of assets held for less than 12 months is treated as income and is subject to income tax. Since such gains will only suffer capital gains tax and not income tax in the UK the exemption section 23(q) mentioned above will not be available and Australian tax liability will arise. A capital loss suffered in the same circumstances will probably not be deductible.

Deductible expenses

The Australian income tax legislation provides that expenditure incurred in deriving exempt income is not deductible.

To the extent that items of expenditure are referable to taxable investment income or capital gains they are deductible. However, it is likely these will be small.

Special reserve fund

Transfers to and from the SRF have no Australian tax consequences. Since the transfers may possibly reduce UK tax liability, there could be an improvement in the net return to Australian names.

Dividends from investments transferred into the SRF will be liable to Australian income tax.

Foreign taxes

Since underwriting profits/losses have no Australian income tax effect double tax relief is not relevant.

Credit will however be given in respect and to the extent of tax paid on dividends and such capital gains as are taxable in Australia. Such credit is limited to the lesser of the Australian and foreign tax.

UK capital gains tax paid is creditable in this respect as are USA, Canadian and other foreign taxes.

Australian returns

An Australian resident individual will normally have a fiscal year ending on 30 June the return for which usually must be lodged by the following 28 February. In the comparatively rare situation of him adopting a 31 December year end the return must be lodged by the following 30 September.

The UK personal accountant should provide Australian resident Name's annually with a taxation advice giving the necessary detailed information for inclusion on his Australian tax return.

This will include details of:

(a) UK and other foreign dividends on special or personal reserve funds;
(b) $3\frac{1}{2}\%$ War Loan interest and any tax free non UK interest;
(c) Capital gains made on assets held for less than 12 months unless subject to income tax in the country of source.

Estate duty

Australia has no estate taxes and there is therefore no possibility of any credit for UK capital transfer tax paid. Care should be taken to minimise such liability by the use of letters of credit or bank guarantees and by limiting investments to those specifically exempted from CTT.

Exchange control

Following a substantial lifting of foreign exchange regulations the issue of a letter of credit or bank guarantee no longer requires approval of the Federal Reserve Bank. Further it is no longer necessary for any income from membership of Lloyd's to be repatriated to Australia.

Guernsey

9.16 *General*

Individuals principally resident in Guernsey are taxed on their world-wide income, whilst individuals resident but not principally resident are taxed only on Guernsey source income and remittances of income to Guernsey. The Administrator of Income Tax in Guernsey agreed in 1981 the basis of assessment for Guernsey tax on Lloyd's income of Names principally resident in Guernsey. This agreement recognises as acceptable the Lloyd's accounting methods.

Underwriting income and gains

Profits are normally taxed on a preceding year basis – that is the profit assessable for a particular year of charge are those earned in the previous year (or accounting period ending in the previous year). However, a Guernsey Name may elect to be assessed on his Lloyd's income on a current year basis. The election once made is irrevocable.

All Lloyd's income, including income from deposits and personal reserves, is charged to income tax. It does not rank as earned income although it is treated as 'business' income.

Although Guernsey has no tax on capital gains or profits the capital appreciation is taxable since such appreciation is viewed as normal commercial profits of the business. However, gains on

UK Government Securities held for more than one year are not assessable to tax.

Deductible expenses

Expenses incurred wholly and exclusively for the purpose of the business are allowed and include:

(a) stop loss premiums (with recoveries treated as business receipts);
(b) loan interest paid or payable;
(c) renewals and maintenance fees on bank guarantees or letters of credit;
(d) accountancy fees;
(e) foreign income taxes.

Special Reserve Fund

The gross equivalent of any transfer into the SRF will be allowed as a deduction in computing the underwriting profit or loss for Guernsey tax. The gross equivalent of any withdrawal will be treated as an income receipt.

Losses

The tax rules for setting off losses in Guernsey vary considerably from the UK rules. In particular, in Guernsey current underwriting losses will be set off against capital appreciation taxable as profits of the business. This may lead to a difference in the amounts of profit suffering UK tax and Guernsey tax in any one year of assessment, with a consequent effect on the amount of double taxation relief available.

Foreign taxes

Relief is granted in respect of UK and foreign taxes paid as follows:

(a) Credit for UK income tax suffered on UK income (apart from UK dividends and debentures) is granted at the full Guernsey effective rate of tax.
(b) US, Canadian and other foreign income taxes suffered are allowed as an expense in arriving at the underwriting profit or loss on the same basis as that allowed in the UK for any year of account.

(c) By concession, credit for UK capital gains tax suffered is granted at the full Guernsey effective rate of tax.

(d) By concession, US and/or Canadian capital gains tax is available for credit against the Guernsey tax liability, but the credit is restricted to the lesser of 75% of the Guernsey effective rate or the actual US/Canadian tax suffered.

Relief at (a), (c) and (d) is restricted by reference to the income actually assessed to Guernsey tax.

Guernsey returns

A return of Lloyd's profit/losses, syndicate investment income and gains is required to be made on a special form within 30 months of the close of an underwriting account (e.g. 1981 Account closed 31 December 1983: return to be made by 30 June 1986). This return should also include agreed liabilities to UK and foreign taxes.

Income and gains arising from the member's Lloyd's deposits and reserves should be returned on a special form with the annual Guernsey Tax Return.

An analysis of syndicate investment income between UK dividends and debenture interest and other sources is strictly required to enable the correct double taxation relief to be calculated. However, the Administrator of Income Tax has recognised the difficulties involved in obtaining such an analysis, and by concession the Name may elect that only 5% of his syndicate investment income be treated as arising from UK dividends and debenture interest.

Estate duty

Guernsey has no estate taxes and no credit for UK capital transfer tax is therefore available. Care should be taken to minimise any CTT liability by the use of letters of credit or bank guarantees and by restricting investments to those specifically exempted from CTT.

Exchange control

For Exchange Control purposes Guernsey is part of the UK Scheduled Territories. It has its own exchange control legislation, identical in effect to the Exchange Control Act 1947 and all exchange control matters are supervised and regulated by the Bank of England. However, following the relaxation announced on 23 October 1979, exchange consent is no longer required for any transactions.

Ireland

9.17 *General*

A domiciled Irish resident is liable to income tax and capital gains tax on all of his income and gains wherever arising. Irish and UK incomes are fully liable in the hands of a resident irrespective of domicile.

Underwriting income and gains

There is an agreement with the Revenue Commissioners in Dublin determining the basis upon which Lloyd's income and gains are to be taxed. This agreement recognises as acceptable the Lloyd's accounting methods and broadly the Name's income as computed for UK tax purposes will be brought into charge to Irish Tax in the same way as for UK tax, e.g. the 1982 underwriting account is assessable for 1982/3.

Also, as in the UK the date of issue of assessments and due dates of payment of tax are delayed and time limits for elections extended to take account of the two year delay in closing the underwriting account.

All capital gains are taxable including those which are exempt in the UK. The Irish indexation and tapering reliefs are not available on syndicate capital gains.

Expenses

All expenses included in the profits computed for UK tax purposes are allowable.

Special Reserve Fund

No tax relief is available for SRF transfers. There are therefore no tax reasons for making transfers to the fund unless there are difficulties in obtaining full credit for UK taxes in the Irish computation.

Foreign taxes

All UK, USA, Canadian and other foreign taxes are available for credit in the Irish tax computation.

Irish tax returns

Each autumn (shortly after the issue of the UK tax advice) syndicate accountants or underwriting agents should provide Irish Name's with an additional tax advice. This will show details of any income which is exempt from UK tax in the hands of the Irish Name (e.g. interest on $3\frac{1}{2}$% War Loan) but liable to Irish tax. The advice will also indicate the amount of any capital gains or losses which are exempt from UK tax (e.g. 'gilts' held for more than 12 months) but subject to Irish tax. Details will already have been included on the normal UK tax advice of gains on which the syndicate has paid tax but which are exempt in the hands of a non UK resident Name. The provision of this information will enable the Name resident in the Republic of Ireland to make the correct Irish tax return.

Estate duty

Inheritance tax is payable by the donee/beneficiary at progressive rates determined by the relationship of the deceased to the successor. To avoid international double taxation there is an estate and gift tax treaty in force with the UK.

Exchange control

(a) Approval is required before a letter of credit/bank guarantee can be established or renewed.
(b) Any income from Lloyd's, net of reserves, must be repatriated to Ireland.

New Zealand

9.18 *General*

All income of an individual resident in New Zealand is taxable at the time that income arises whether it is derived from New Zealand or elsewhere. However the New Zealand Income Tax Act provides that for underwriters income from underwriting subjected to tax outside New Zealand is exempt to tax in New Zealand.

Capital gains are in any event not taxable in New Zealand.

Underwriting income and gains

Most Lloyd's income being subejct to tax in the UK is exempt to tax in New Zealand. This includes underwriting profits, syndicate investment income and capital appreciation. It also includes interest and dividends arising on investments in the Lloyd's Special or Personal Reserve funds.

The exemption will not however apply to 3½% War Loan interest since that is exempt to UK tax when due to a New Zealand resident.

Expenses

Since the income is exempt no expense can be deducted.

Special Reserve Fund

Transfers to and from the SRF have no New Zealand tax consequences as it is dealing with exempt income. If UK tax can be reduced by making transfers this could be of advantage to New Zealand Name's.

Foreign taxes

Since underwriting income and gains have no New Zealand income tax effect double taxation relief is not relevant.

New Zealand tax returns

The UK personal accountant should provide New Zealand resident Name's annually with a taxation advice giving the necessary detailed information for inclusion on his New Zealand return.

Exchange gains/losses

As Lloyd's profit is derived outside New Zealand exchange gains and losses are not to be included.

Estate duty

If a person is resident (domiciled) in New Zealand at the time of death then any property situated outside New Zealand is included in his dutiable estate. Where overseas duty is paid on assets situated outside New Zealand some relief if allowed.

UK capital transfer tax can be minimised by use of letters of credit or bank guarantees and limiting investments to those specifically exempted.

Exchange control

(a) Membership of Lloyd's requires approval by the Reserve Bank of New Zealand.
(b) The contribution to annual membership requires Reserve Bank approval but this is a technical requirement only.
(c) Payment to fund losses is allowed but evidence may be required before funds are remitted overseas.

Any income from membership of Lloyd's must be repatriated to New Zealand.

South Africa

9.19 *General*

South African residents are only liable for normal income tax arising from, or deemed to arise from, sources within the Republic of South Africa.

Underwriting income and gains

All Lloyd's income and gains are exempt from tax in South Africa being income arising from sources outside South Africa.

Expenses

Since the income is exempt no expenses can be claimed.

Special Reserve Fund

Transfers to and from the SRF have no South African tax consequences. If UK tax can be reduced by making transfers, this could be of advantage to South African Names.

Foreign taxes

Since underwriting income and gains have no South African income tax effect, double taxation relief is not relevant.

Capital/estate duty

If a deceased Name were ordinarily resident in South Africa at the time of death then in certain circumstances assets situated in the UK as a result of Lloyd's membership could result in estate duty being payable in South Africa on those assets.

To relieve international double taxation there is a UK–South Africa tax treaty in force

UK capital transfer tax can be minimised by use of letters of credit or bank guarantees and limiting investments to those specifically exempted.

Exchange control

Approval of the Reserve Bank of South Africa is required for South African residents to participate at Lloyd's. In addition, any profits arising from membership are required to be remitted to South Africa unless retained in the UK with South African Reserve Bank permission.

10 Tax consequences of an investment in Lloyd's

10.1 Since the results of a Name's Lloyd's syndicates are reported three years after the year for which they are assessed, tax planning is limited. Many taxpayers ignore the syndicate profits (or losses), investment income and capital gains in planning the alleviation of their taxes. This simplistic approach has its advantages:

(a) unnecessary professional charges are not incurred where these relate to seeking tax shelters in excess of the aggregate of non-Lloyd's income and income from personal Lloyd's reserves and deposits which may not be usable due to poor underwriting results;

(b) the transfers to Special Reserve Fund limit the effect of higher and until 1983–84 additional rate taxes;

(c) the sums received from Lloyd's may be regarded as additional spending money, to be used for holidays etc, as the Name already has other income which satisfies his needs.

10.2 If the Name regards Lloyd's as an investment, which effectively gives a double return on the money 'invested' in the Lloyd's deposit, some planning is advisable. In the following paragraphs certain suggestions are made. These show the advantages of becoming a Name at Lloyd's as well as referring to the tax position.

10.3 At least 25 per cent of the money invested in the Lloyd's deposit must be in cash or British Government securities with a life of not more than five years. Normally, if a high marginal rate of tax is payable on other income, the Name will arrange to invest in low-interest rate stocks, with a potential capital gain, rather than in high-yielders with little scope for capital gain. When interest rates are likely to fall, it may be sensible to invest in high yielding stocks and sell them cum interest. The resulting gain may be larger even though the accrued interest will after 28

February 1986 be treated as income. But even if the interest is received, the tax on 50 per cent of it is limited to 30 per cent (subject to the maximum gross limit of £7,000 on transfers to the Special Reserve Fund). Unless the capital gains made by a tax-payer are likely to be less than the annual exemption, the interest, bearing tax at only 30 per cent, suffers the same rate as capital gains.

10.4   A similar view may be taken in respect of investing in equities. The purchase of shares, regarded as high yielding, may ultimately give rise to substantial capital gains. While awaiting such gains the one half of the dividends transferred to Special Reserve Fund will suffer a maximum tax rate of 30 per cent.

10.5   As indicated earlier, the building up of funds in the Special Reserve Fund increases future capital resources, on which income arises which will itself be available for transfer. If the maximum is transferred annually, the Name will build up an increasing fund which will help to provide income following his retirement from his main occupation. It can be treated as a 'second pension fund', which with a good investment policy may provide some security against inflation following retirement. It must be admitted it may not be as safe as one from an approved pension scheme since underwriting losses can arise. When the Name dies or retires, it is an amount equal to the amount trans-ferred which is charged to income tax. Any surpluses arising from good investment will in the case of death be exempt from income and capital gains tax; on resignation the surpluses will pass free of capital gains tax (see **8.9** and **8.12**).

10.6   As indicated in **8.15** business relief at the rate of 50 per cent is available when computing liabilities to capital transfer tax. Normally, the assets comprising the Lloyd's deposit, reserves, and outstanding year's results should not devolve on the Name's spouse since such transfers are exempt from that tax. It is usually advisable to seek to provide the spouse with other assets. The assets in the Lloyd's deposit etc, could pass to the children, who, where the nil rate band applies up to £67,000, will be able to receive assets of £134,000 free of capital transfer tax. So that assets can pass immediately to the beneficiaries and not wait for three years while accounts are settled, it is advisable to take out a special policy. A Name can obtain details from his underwriting agent. Effectively, the policy provides Lloyd's with a guarantee to meet any losses which may arise while settling the accounts, thus allowing the legal personal representatives to assent to transferring assets to beneficiaries.

10.7   The spouse, if not already a Name, should be given other assets, either during lifetime or in the will. During life, the Name can arrange through his or her underwriting agent that his or her spouse can take their place.

10.8   If both spouses are Names, they should leave their Lloyd's interests to their children and not to each other. The business relief will apply to both their interests, thus increasing the value of their estates to be passed to their dependants.

10.9   Since claims for business expansion relief under section 26 of the Finance Act 1983 must be made within two years, it is not possible to await the declaration of the Lloyd's results before deciding whether to invest under the scheme. However, in view of the time limits relief under section 30 of the Finance Act 1978, in respect of losses in a new enterprise which may be set against Lloyd's income (see **4.13**). It may be sensible for the spouse having the Lloyd's income to be the trader or partner claiming relief under that section. The other spouse will claim business expansion relief.

10.10   Since many claims take years to settle and premiums are being received throughout the year, many syndicates can invest substantial sums. Capital gains made thereon may have suffered tax or as being from Government Securities exempt so that on receipt the funds are available for further investment or the creation of additional personal reserves at Lloyd's; thus enabling further building of capital resources, which, subject to agreement with the Inland Revenue, will be available for business relief in computing capital transfer tax liabilities.

10.11   For Working Names, the transfers to Special Reserve Fund create further capital resources on which income will be received. Further capital resources enable or which will enable them to increase the level of premium income which may be underwritten. Providing profits increase, they will be able to increase their retirement annuity payments. Thus, they obtain a double benefit: the creation of capital out of income, and the ability to create a bigger pension safe from underwriting losses.

10.12   For non-residents, an interest in Lloyd's creates a spread of wealth outside their own countries, including an interest in the American economy. For UK residents there is exposure to overseas investments in other economies.

10.13 The tax consequences have been set out in this chapter as they are a factor in deciding whether becoming a Name is worth the commercial risk of unlimited liability.

11   Inland Revenue investigation at Lloyd's

11.1   The taxation of Names is at the present time much confused by the investigations which the Inland Revenue are making into the taxation of the syndicates. These investigations stem initially from the publication of the actions of directors of managing agents of certain syndicates at Lloyd's and are being conducted not by Leeds (Underwriters Unit) but by the Special Investigation Section of the Inland Revenue. The scope and conduct of these enquiries is outside the subject matter of this book but broadly the investigations centre on certain types of reinsurance contracts and on the closing provisions carried forward annually in respect of claims (the reinsurance to close). On 6 April 1984 the Inland Revenue wrote to managing agents in the following terms:

Dear Sirs

In respect of syndicates managed by your agency will you please let me have, within the next 30 days, all documents, correspondence and other information relevant to arrangements which have existed at any time since 6 April 1974 purporting to be contracts of reinsurance if:

a. under the terms of the contract documents, or
b. by any addenda, or
c. by any associated letter of intent or related agreement, or
d. by any other understanding

either

(i)   amounts substantially equivalent to the 'premiums' paid are or were to be returned ultimately to the syndicate in one way or another whether with or without an addition for income arising from the investment of these 'premiums', or
(ii)   the indemnity or the maximum sum recoverable cannot or could not materially exceed the 'premiums' payable plus any amounts carried forward from previous arrangements plus the income arising from the investment of those 'premiums' and amounts.

Any contract under which the amount recoverable by the syndicate cannot be less than 60% of the 'premiums' payable by the syndicate should be treated as falling within (i) above for the purpose of this letter.

If no such arrangements exist or have existed please confirm this to be so.

Yours faithfully

J A HUCKVALE

The investigations go on and will probably continue to do so for some time. It may be that ultimately assessments will be taken to appeal.

11.2   The immediate practical effect on the personal taxation of Names is that matters cannot be finalised because the Inland Revenue have in the case of many syndicates not felt able to agree the computations for the 1980 and 1981 underwriting accounts and moreover have felt it necessary to protect their position by raising protective estimated assessments for the tax year 1976/77 before that year went out of date for assessment.

11.3   The method adopted for the 1980 account was set out in a notice issued by Leeds Underwriters Unit on 2 December 1983 in the following terms:

IMPORTANT NOTICE

UNDERWRITING ACCOUNT 1980 (CLOSED 31 DECEMBER 1982)

This notice contains important information relating to your profits or losses for Income Tax purposes for the Underwriting Account 1980 (closed 31 December 1982) and should be read in conjunction with the form LL9 for that year. It explains that the profits or losses for Income Tax purposes for certain syndicates have been estimated and tells you what you should do if you wish to appeal against an assessment which includes those figures, or to make a loss relief claim, or to make a payment into the Special Reserve Fund. These special arrangements apply for the 1980 Account only and should not be regarded as creating a precedent for future years.

Underwriting Profits and Losses as Adjusted for Income Tax Purposes
The underwriting profits or losses adjusted for Income Tax purposes for certain syndicates of which you are a member have not yet been agreed by me and there is likely to be some considerable delay before they are agreed. It has therefore been necessary for me to use estimated figures for your shares of the profits or losses of those syndicates. As a result, the net total for the Case I profit or loss from your

underwriting business for Account 1980, as shown on the form LL9, contains an estimated element.

Income Tax Assessments for 1980/81
Where the form LL9 shows a net Case I profit, assessments at the Basic Rate – and later at the higher rates – will be made using that figure. If you decide to appeal against those assessments – on the grounds that the amount assessed is higher than the aggregate of your shares in the syndicate profits and losses – and wish to postpone payment of so much of the tax as relates to the excess, you should make an application to me as explained in the notes accompanying the Notice of Assessment.

Relief for Losses
Where the form LL9 shows a net Case I loss, until that figure is finally determined, any repayment resulting from a loss relief claim will be provisional only and will be restricted to the lesser of 75% of the Case I loss shown on form LL9, or your syndicate investment income. If the net Case I loss exceeds the syndicate investment income and the balance of your Special Reserve Funds is less than 7/10ths of the excess, the repayment will be restricted to 75% of the net Case I loss, less 10/7ths of the balance of your Special Reserve Funds.

Special Reserve Funds
It will not be possible for me to agree the amount of the payment into the Special Reserve Funds for the 1980 Underwriting Year until the Case I profit or loss from your underwriting business for that year is finally determined. You may, however, make payments into the Fund if you wish provisional relief to be taken into account in the Higher Rate Tax Assessment, to be made in the first half of 1984.

If you wish to proceed in this way, you should notify me in the normal way, not later than six weeks from the date of issue of form LL9, of the amount to be paid into the Funds. The amount, when grossed up, should not exceed the lesser of £7000 or 50% of the profit as defined for Special Reserve Fund purposes. In arriving at the profit for this purpose, you should use the figures shown on form LL9. Provisional relief will not be given until payment has actually been made.

The position when the Case I profit or loss from your underwriting business has been finally determined will then be as follows:

(a) If the profit, as defined for Special Reserve Fund purposes, is increased, you will be allowed to make a further payment into the Funds, provided that the total of all payments into the Funds for the year does not, when grossed up, exceed the lesser of £7000 or 50% of the final profit for Special Reserve Fund purposes.

(b) If the profit as defined for Special Reserve Fund purposes is reduced, relief for Income Tax purposes will be restricted to the lesser of £7000 or 50% of the profit as defined for Special

Reserve Fund purposes. Any payment already made into the Fund which is then found to be excessive will be treated as if it were an advance payment for the next year in which there is a profit for Special Reserve Fund purposes, unless in practice the excess is withdrawn.

If the aggregate of the amounts apportioned to you by the syndicates of which you are a member is a loss, as defined for Special Reserve Fund purposes, the provisional withdrawal procedure will operate in the normal way. Final determination of the amount to be withdrawn will not however be possible until the Case I profit or loss from your underwriting business has been finally determined.

C J Wannop
District Inspector
Leeds (Underwriters Unit)

What happened in practice is that where an entry or form LL9 would on the basis of the unagreed computations have shown a profit that profit was rounded up to the nearest £1000. Where the computation would have shown a loss that loss was rounded down to the nearest £1000. Repayments were then restricted as set out in the Revenue Statement and Special Reserve Fund transfers were based on provisional figures. The tax position of many Names therefore remain open for the 1980 account and will not be resolved until the enquiries are settled.

11.4 Similar considerations applied to the syndicate computations for the 1981 account. The Inland Revenue made relatively arbitrary adjustments to the computations submitted by the syndicate accountants which could have the effect of increasing a profit, reducing a loss or converting a loss into a profit. The treatment adopted was set out in a notice issued by Inland Revenue in the following terms:

IMPORTANT NOTICE

UNDERWRITING ACCOUNT 1981 (CLOSED 31 DECEMBER 1983)

This notice contains important information relating to your profits or losses for income tax purposes for the Underwriting Account 1981 (closed 31 December 1983) and should be read in conjunction with the form LL9 for that year. It explains that the profits or losses for income tax purposes for certain syndicates have been estimated and tells you what you should do if you wish to appeal against an assessment which includes estimates, or to make a loss relief claim, or to make a payment into the Special Reserve Fund. These special arrangements apply for the 1981 Account only and should not be regarded as creating a precedent for future years.

Underwriting Profits and Losses as Adjusted for Income Tax Purposes
The underwriting profits or losses adjusted for income tax purposes for certain syndicates of which you are a member have not been agreed by me and there is likely to be some considerable delay before they are agreed. I have therefore used estimated figures for your shares of the profits or losses for those syndicates. Generally the profits have been increased or the losses restricted by reference to the premiums paid by the syndicate concerned during 1981 on policies which are the subject of enquiry by the Revenue. Those figures which are estimated are marked E on the form LL9.

Income Tax Assessments for 1981/82
Where the form LL9 shows a net Case I profit, assessments at the Basic Rate – and later at the higher rates – will be made using that figure. If you decide to appeal against those assessments – on the grounds that the amount assessed is higher than the aggregate of your shares in the syndicate profits and losses – and wish to postpone payment of so much of the tax as relates to the excess, you should make an application to me as explained in the notes accompanying the Notice of Assessment.

Relief for Losses
Where the form LL9 shows a net Case I loss only provisional relief will be allowed in respect of that loss. It will be restricted to the lesser of the Case I loss shown on form LL9 or of your syndicate investment income. Provisional relief computed on this basis may only be claimed by repayment of the Basic Rate tax suffered on your syndicate investment income, or by set-off against the higher rate tax subsequently due on that income.

The following note was issued to Agents by the manager of the Legislation and Taxation Department of Lloyd's.

To all Agents

1981 ACCOUNT: YEAR-END TAX ARRANGEMENTS

The results of many syndicates for 1981 year of account will be estimated for tax purposes (1981/82 year of assessment).

The tax assessments on a great many Names will, therefore, contain estimates.

The Revenue will issue a notice of explanation (copy attached) with the LL9's, which should be issued between mid-October and mid-November, explaining the procedures which it is applying in such cases. These procedures are re-stated in the letter to assist you in understanding the proposals and in advising your Name.

(1) Syndicate underwriting results for 1981 account will be estimated for tax in many cases.

(2) Most, but by no means all, of the estimates will be made in cases where there has been charged in syndicate accounts a premium on a policy of the sort described in the Revenue's general letter of enquiry dated 6 April 1984.

(3) In most, but by no means all cases the estimate will be made by adding to the syndicate profit (or by deducting from the syndicate loss) the amount of the premium referred to at (2). In other cases the estimate will be made by the exercise of the Inspector's best judgement.

(4) Estimated figures will be identified on the LL9 by the letter 'E'.

(5) Where the Name has an overall underwriting profit which includes an estimated figure of profit or loss in one or more syndicates, the assessment on that profit is subject to appeal in the ordinary way ie the appeal should be made within 30 days of issue of the assessment on the grounds that it is estimated.

If the Name wishes to seek postponement of tax on the estimated element he should make that application at the same time.

(6) Where the Name has an overall underwriting loss which includes an estimated figure of profit or loss on one or more syndicates claims for loss relief will be admitted by the Revenue on a provisional basis only until the figures are finally and formally agreed.

(7) Provisional relief will be available on the full amount of the underwriting loss as shown by the LL9 as reduced by any provisional SRF withdrawals. Relief will, however, be available only against tax on 1981 account syndicate investment income. Relief will not be available against any other income of 1981/82 year of assessment nor against any income of any other year.

(8) When loss figures are finally and formally agreed with the Revenue the Name may claim loss relief against other income of 1981/82 or against income of other years under the normal loss relief provisions. The repayment then made will take into account any provisional relief or repayment given and the normal rules of repayment supplement will apply.

(9) Provisional relief against tax on 1981 syndicate investment income will be given:

(a) by repayment of basic rate tax due on 1 January 1985 *and*
(b) by reduction of higher rate tax due on 1 July 1985.

(10) Where the Name's overall underwriting profit or loss does not include any estimated figures the normal SRF rules will apply.

(11) Where, however, there is an estimated element the following procedures will apply:

(a) Where there is a profit, payment into SRF may be made, on the basis of the LL9 figures, on a provisional basis.

Notice of the intention to make a payment into SRF must be given to the Inspector not later than 31 December 1984.

Higher rate relief will not be given unless there is an actual payment into the fund.

When the profit is finally agreed with the Revenue further payments may, if the profit is increased, be made into SRF, or withdrawals may be made if the profit is decreased (or the excess may be treated as a payment in advance for later years).

If the final agreement is such that a loss becomes profit payment into SRF will be allowed notwithstanding that notice of intention to transfer was not given to the Inspector by 31 December 1984.

(b) Where there is a loss, withdrawal from SRF will be allowed on a provisional basis, at 50% of the loss as computed for SRF purposes, incorporating in this calculation the loss as shown on the LL9.

Full withdrawal will not be possible until figures are finally agreed with the Inspector but representations may be made to the Revenue in exceptional cases eg of hardship.

Yours faithfully

K S Goddard
Manager
Legislation & Taxation Department

Once again therefore there is an unresolved tax situation. There has since been a relaxation of the rules dealing with provisional repayments for 1981. Further repayments are being made up to 75% of the loss less ten-sevenths of the balance in the SRF (after allowing for provisional withdrawals). This relaxation has allowed a provisional set off against other income of 1981/82 but claims under section 30 of the Finance Act 1978 are not being accepted at time of writing.

11.5 At the time of writing it is not known what the position will be for the 1982 account. It may well be however, that similar estimated assessments will be made with restriction of loss reliefs and provisional SRF transfers. If that is the case it will be necessary for accountants acting for Names to appeal against any estimated assessments and if the result is a Case I loss to tell the Revenue that the figure is not agreed. Consideration will also need to be given to whether payment of tax charged should be postponed. Bearing in mind that interest could arise if the payment on account falls short of the ultimate liability it may be prudent either to pay the whole of the tax charged or to pay the tax which would have been due by reference to the original computations and buy certificates of tax deposit to cover the balance. This is a matter to be decided in individual cases.

11.6 At the end of March 1985 the Inland Revenue issued estimated assessments on many Names for 1976/77. Names will have been advised to appeal against these assessments and have decided whether to pay the tax charged. The corollary to the Revenue argument that certain reinsurance premiums may not be allowable deductions is that corresponding reinsurance proceeds may not be taxable receipts. Names should therefore have made an 'error or mistake' claim for 1976/77 on the grounds that tax may have been overpaid because of an error or mistake in their tax return. Similar action may need to be taken for 1977/78 and future years if the Inland Revenue again make protective assessments.

11.7 It was announced on the 15th October that the Inland Revenue and Lloyds have reached a settlement under which £42.5m. will be paid from Lloyd's central funds together with interest from the 1st August in respect of past tax liabilities which the Revenue alleges are due. However, certain members of the market whom the Revenue considers took actions which 'turned towards criminality' are not the subject of the settlement. Moreover Names on certain syndicates where the Revenue is arguing over matters not dealt with in the central settlement, which covered roll-over policies, time and distance policies and re-insurance to close, may find that enquiries continue.

Appendices

Appendix 1

Form of letter to US Name giving details of items to be shown on his US tax return.

Letterhead of
LLOYD'S PANEL ACCOUNTANT

Dear Sir,

We set out below the information you require in respect of your participation in Lloyd's Syndicates for purposes of your 1977 US Federal income tax return. All figures shown are in US dollars.

I	UNDERWRITING RESULTS	1977	1978 Estimate
	1974 Account Released during 1977		
	Gross premiums (less returns)		
	Business expenses, losses including reinsurance ceded		
	Profit (Loss)	_____	
	US Source	_____	
	Profit (Loss)		
	Non-US Source	_____	
	Profit (Loss)	_____	

II	INVESTMENT INCOME		
A	LLOYD'S AMERICAN TRUST FUND (US Source except as indicated)	1977	1978 Estimates
	Taxable Interest		
	Tax Exempt Interest (States to be specified)		
	Dividends		
	Net Long Term Gain (Loss)		
	Net Short Term Gain (Loss)		
B	LLOYD'S STERLING TRUST FUND (Non-US Source except as indicated)		
	Interest		
	Dividends		
	Net Long Term Gain (Loss)		
	Net Short Term Gain (Loss)		
C	PERSONAL FUND INVESTMENTS	US Source	Non-US Source
	Interest		
	Dividends		
	Net Long Term Gain (Loss)		
	Net Short Term Gain (Loss)		

III FOREIGN INCOME TAXES PAID DURING 1977

The foreign income taxes paid, consisted of the following

(a) Income tax paid to the United Kingdom and capital gains tax $_____

(b) Income tax withheld in Canada _____

(c) Income taxes paid elsewhere _____

Yours faithfully,

117

Appendix 2

UNITED STATES MEMBERS OF LLOYD'S

NAME:_____

Syndicate Accountant:_____

Lloyd's Syndicate Investment Income and Capital Gains Year 1979/80
Lloyd's Deposit Fiscal Year 1981/82

Syndicate Nos.							TOTAL
£	£	£	£	£	£	£	
Name's Syndicate Investment Income (Allocated to 1979 Account) Total Worldwide as per Form LL 185 L.A.T.F. Element Interest & Dividends Illinois & Kentucky Element Interest							
Name's Syndicate Capital gains (Allocated to 1979 Account) Total Worldwide L.A.T.F. Illinois & Kentucky Element Canadian Element Foreign and Exempt Securities UK Government Securities (Sec. 99 ICTA 1970) US $ Calendar Year Premium Income 1981							
Total Worldwide Calendar Year Premium Income 1981							
Block Reserves Held by the Agent— 1981/82							
Nominal Amount of Reserves Interest (i) UK Securities (ii) US Securities Dividends (i) UK Securities (ii) US Securities Capital Gains on which UK tax has been paid (i) US Securities (ii) Foreign and Exempt Securities (iii) UK Government Securities (Sec. 99 ICTA 1970)							

Interest on reserves received without deduction of United Kingdom tax at source
amounted to £

Interest of £   on reserve investments of £   is exempt
from UK Tax

Signed...Syndicate Accountant.

LL60 (Section 'A')

118

UNITED STATES MEMBERS OF LLOYD'S

NAME_____

PERSONAL UK TAX ACCOUNTANT_____

Fiscal Year 1981/82	Lloyd's Deposits	Special Reserves	Personal Reserves	TOTAL
	£	£	£	£
Nominal Amount of Deposit/Reserve				
Part Secured by Letter of Credit				
Interest (i) UK Securities				
(ii) US Securities				
Dividends (i) UK Securities				
(ii) US Securities				
Capital Gains on which UK Tax has been paid				
(i) US Securities				
(ii) Foreign and Exempt Securities				
(iii) US Government Securities (Section 99 ICTA 1970)				

Interest on deposits and reserves received without deduction of United Kigndom tax at source amounted to £

Interest of £   on deposit and reserve investments of £
is exempt from UK tax.

Signed ....Personal Accountant

LL60 (Section 'B')

Appendix 3

Address ....

....

....

....

Date ....

H.M. Inspector of Taxes.
Leeds (Underwriters Unit)

Ref:

Dear Sir,

As a United States Resident Name, I hereby elect to take relief
under the 'special arrangement' dated June, 1973 with effect from
the year of assessment ....

Yours faithfully,

Signed ....

Full Name ....

Appendix 4

TELEPHONE 01-623 7100
EXTENSION No. 2477
TELEGRAMS: LLOYDS LONDON EC3
TELEX 886691 LLOYDS LDN
PLEASE QUOTE REFERENCE—FC

LLOYD'S
LIME STREET,
LONDON,
EC3M 7HA.
27th March, 1975

Dear Sirs,

Finance Act, 1974—Tax Relief on Interest Paid

The law on what constitutes allowable interest for tax purposes has been changed again by the Finance Act 1974. Discussions have taken place with the Revenue to examine the particular problems of Members.

The attached circular deals with interest on loans to fund losses. As to interest on money borrowed to finance Lloyd's Deposits (and Premiums Trust Fund Deposits) the Revenue are still willing to accept claims for interest relief by Members actively engaged in the business of Lloyd's where it is shown that the borrowing was undertaken to finance those deposits. The Revenue is however unable to give such relief to Members who are not actively engaged in the business of Lloyd's.

The Members entitled to relief will be those actively engaged in the business of Lloyd's and employed full time either in the Room at Lloyd's or in the office of an Underwriting Agent or Lloyd's Broker during the fiscal year of claim.

Your faithfully,

Finance Comptroller

This letter has been sent to all Underwriting Agents, Active Underwriters and Panel Auditors.

FINANCE ACT 1974

TAXATION RELIEF FOR LLOYD'S UNDERWRITERS ON INTEREST ON MONEY BORROWED TO FINANCE UNDERWRITING LOSSES

AGREEMENT WITH INLAND REVENUE

I. BRIEF SUMMARY OF FINANCE ACT 1974 PROVISIONS

The Finance Act 1974 has, broadly speaking, substituted the Finance Act 1969 provisions on interest paid by individuals for those of the Finance Act 1972. The effects of the new provisions are that:

1. Interest on money borrowed after 26 March 1974 is eligible for relief only if the borrowing is for business or other specified purposes. Non-business overdraft or similar credit card interest however, is not eligible for relief except where the transitional arrangements apply in respect of debts in existence on 26 March 1974.

2. In the case of a fixed debt in existence at 26 March 1974 which does not qualify for relief under the new provisions, transitional relief will be given for interest payable up to 5 April 1982.

3. In the case of non-business overdrafts in existence on 26 March 1974, relief will continue for interest payable before 6 April 1975 but will be limited to the amount of interest that would be payable after 26 March 1974 and before 6 April 1975 on the overdraft on 26 March 1974 at the rate applicable on that date. The relief will be given however, only when such interest is actually paid.

The relief for interest on new loans within (1) above is the full amount of the interest, whereas there is no relief for the first £35 interest on loans within (2) and (3) above.

In the case of non-business overdrafts in existence on 26 March 1974, Members should have converted them into fixed loans before 6 April 1975 in order to extend the transitional relief to interest payable before 6 April 1982. Relief for the loan interest however, will be limited to that which would be payable on a loan equal to the overdraft on 26 March 1974.

II. INTEREST CHARGED BY UNDERWRITING AGENT AND CREDITED TO SYNDICATE FUNDS.

Interest charged by a Syndicate on a Member's unfunded loss and credited to Syndicate funds is to be dealt with as follows:

Interest credited in the calendar year to Syndicate funds in this manner will be allocated to underwriting accounts in that calendar year and included accordingly in the Syndicate Interest Income Tax assessment.

It has been agreed with City 18 Leeds (now Leeds Underwriting Unit) that the interest paid by a member to a Syndicate will qualify for tax relief as follows:

(a) Interest charged to a Member for a calendar year is to be deducted from his share of Syndicate Investment Income for the underwriting year closing at the end of that calendar year. The net amount remaining will represent his syndicate investment income for that underwriting year. The interest charged and set-off in this manner is to be paid net after deducting basic rate tax.

(b) In so far as the interest charged exceeds the Member's share of Syndicate Investment Income in the circumstances described above, that excess is to be charged gross before deduction of basic rate tax. For tax relief purposes the amount charged gross is deductible as an expense in the Member's underwriting Schedule D Case I figure for the underwriting year closing at the end of the calendar year for which the interest has been charged. Alternatively relief for interest paid gross may be claimed under Section 75 of the Finance Act 1972, subject to the restrictions contained in the Finance Act 1974.

In the case of those syndicates where interest received is exceptionally assessed under Case I, the interest paid in any year will be treated as a deduction in arriving at the Case I profit or loss for that syndicate for the underwriting account closing at the end of that year.

III. INTEREST ON BORROWED MONEY

1. GENERAL

a. It is agreed that tax relief should be given for interest paid by a Member of Lloyd's on money borrowed to finance the net amount paid into his syndicate to meet underwriting losses or open year deficiencies.

b.   For taxation purposes the combined results of all the syndicates in which a Member underwrites constitute a single business activity and it is necessary to take into account that he may have profits in one syndicate and losses in another.

c.   In deciding how long relief should continue, it is necessary to take into account that losses in one year may be followed by profits in subsequent years. The borrowing should be reduced by subsequent profits.

d.   It is also necessary to take into account that borrowing to finance underwriting losses may be part only of a Member's total borrowing and that this may be from more than one source and at differing rates of interest.

e.   The arrangements in the following paragraphs therefore set out the maximum borrowing for which relief will be given and the maximum rate of interest. Relief will be given on the lower of (a) the amount of interest calculated in accordance with the arrangements or (b) the actual interest paid.

f.   In order to avoid undue complications and minute calculations, certain rule of thumb measurements are used in the arrangements.

2.   BASIS OF COMPUTATION

a.   The 'qualifying' amount of borrowing for any year will be the accumulated net losses, as defined below, at the beginning of the year plus or minus the 'adjusted' losses or 'adjusted' profits for the year.

b.   A profit or loss for any one year is the sum of the results for all the syndicates in which a Member participates.

c.   A loss for the purpose of these arrangements is the amount which the Member has funded to his agent in cash, whether from his own resources, from borrowings or from his Premiums Trust Fund Deposit, Reserves or Special Reserve Fund, in respect of a closed year loss or an open year audit deficiency.

d.   A profit is defined as the Member's share of the balance on a closed underwriting account which is for this purpose to be the profit for the year just closed including underwriting profit, investment income (before tax) and appreciation (before tax) for that year of account less all expenses including any interest debited to the personal account for the year just ended.

N.B.   i. No deduction should be made for any amounts retained by the agent by way of personal reserves.

     ii. A deduction should be made for any amount retained—
       (a) To release the earmarking of a Premium Trust Fund Deposit, Reserve or Special Reserve investment previously earmarked for audit purposes against an underwriting loss which reduced the amount the Name was required to fund.
       (b) Against an open year audit deficiency.

    iii. An addition should be made for amounts paid in previous years to meet open year deficiencies and available for release following the close of the account.

e. In order to define the qualifying borrowing for a year it is necessary to define when profits are paid out and when losses are funded as the amount of the borrowing will not be constant throughout the year. For the purposes of this arrangement (i) profits will be deemed to be paid out on 30 June and will therefore reduce the borrowing for half the year and (ii) losses will be deemed to be funded on the 1st day of the month in which they are in fact funded. For example:

		Qualifying Amount
Cumulative borrowing at start of year	£10,000	£10,000
Profit for year from syndicate 1 (deemed to be paid out 30 June)	2,000 for ½ year	1,000
	8,000	9,000
Loss for year funded to syndicate 2 on 15 May	1,500 for $^8/_{12}$ year	1,000
Cumulative total carried forward to following year	£ 9,500	Relief based on £10,000

f. Since a Member's borrowings to finance underwriting losses may be only a part of his total borrowings from several sources and at varying rates of interest, it is necessary to apply a 'standard' interest rate to the qualifying borrowing in order to arrive at the maximum amount of interest which will rank for relief. The 'standard' rate of interest will be 2% over the average of the base

125

rate of the National Westminster Bank Ltd for the year in question.

g. The Inland Revenue reserve the right to review the method of arriving at the 'standard' rate of interest if the interest rate structure changes and the margins between that base rate and borrowing rates vary.

h. The product of applying the 'standard' rate of interest to the qualifying borrowing will be the maximum on which relief will be given. Certificates of interest paid to a bank etc. will have to be produced to the Inland Revenue and if this amounts to less than the amount computed in accordance with these arrangements, relief will be restricted to the amount actually paid.

i. Interest paid by executors or by a ceased Underwriter for the period between date of death or cessation and the normal closing date for the last account in which he participated will be treated as admissible. In addition:

a. where a syndicate is not running off, any interest paid in the year following the close of the account will be treated as an admissible charge for the last year of account.

b. where a syndicate is running off, interest paid up to 12 months after the year in which the account is finally closed or 12 months after the Name reinsures himself out of the run off, will continue to be admissible. The year of assessment for which relief will be allowed will follow the procedures applicable to running off syndicates; for example, interest paid in 1975 will qualify for relief in 1973/74, or if the running off account is finally closed on 31 December 1975 any admissible interest paid in 1976 would be treated as relating to the last year of the run off, that is 1975 and would qualify for relief in 1973/74.

The figure of qualifying borrowing on the claim form will be the amount as at 31 December next following the normal closing date, less deposits released during the preceding 12 months or still held by agents at that date, other than those retained in connection with the running off syndicate.

IV. TIMING OF RELIEF

Interest paid outside the syndicate will be allocated to the year of account closing at the end of that year, for example, interest paid in 1975 will be deducted in the Case I computation for 1973 assessable in 1973/74.

V. METHOD OF CLAIMING RELIEF

a.   The information required to claim relief can be collated only by the Member's personal tax adviser.

b.   Printed claim forms will be provided in due course by H.M. Inspector of Taxes, City 18 (Leeds), (now Leeds Underwriting Unit) to whom they should be returned after completion.

c.   Attached is a specimen form to be used by syndicate agents in providing a Member's personal tax adviser with necessary details for completion of the claim form.

d.   As a result of the three year account system there will be two sets of rules for claiming relief for interest paid until 31 December 1975. The provisions of the Finance Act 1972 set out in my letter of 27 April 1973, will apply to the underwriting years 1972 and 1973. The provisions of the Finance Act 1974 as set out in this paper will apply from underwriting year 1974.

e.   It will be noted that, as mentioned in III. 2. c., the maximum relief is related to the amount of the loss funded in cash. It is not reduced by either releases from the Special Reserve Fund, Free Reserves or Premiums Trust Fund Deposits, nor is it reduced by subsequent recoveries of tax. Similarly, subsequent profits which go towards reducing the qualifying borrowing cannot therefore be reduced by tax liabilities or amounts retained by underwriting agents to set up free reserves, although profits may be reduced to the extent that they are utilised to release Funds earmarked for earlier losses.

VI. TRANSITIONAL PROVISIONS

a.   Under the Finance Act 1972, the first £35 of interest paid is disallowed as a deduction unless it is for 'protected interest' (which is not applicable to loans to finance deposits or losses) or is allowed as a business expense. This provision continues to apply until relief ceases, where applicable, for bank overdraft interest (up to 5 April 1975) and for loan interest (up to 5 April 1982).

Relief can be claimed under the 1972 Act provisions up to 5 April 1975, or 1982, as appropriate, with the loss of relief for the first £35 of interest on borrowings to finance the Lloyd's deposits by a Lloyd's Name, which is not regarded as a business expense under the 1972 legislation.

Alternatively relief may be sought for interest on money borrowed by Lloyd's Names to finance deposits within the above rules for interest on money borrowed to finance losses.

b. Interest paid in 1974 is chargeable against the second assessment for 1972/73.

c. Members may find it more convenient to claim relief for interest for one year, i.e. 1974, subject to the £35 restriction rather than to collect all the information for form LL19.

Note: the letter originally referred to interest relief claimable up to 5 April 1980. This date has been altered to 1982 in view of the provisions of the Finance (No. 2) Act 1979.

Certificate of Underwriting Profits and Payments to Meet Underwriting Losses as required for the purposes of a claim to relief for interest paid.

We as underwriting agents for ....

a Member of Lloyd's, certify that

(a) The following amounts were received from the Member to fund underwriting losses.

	No.	*Amount*	*Date*
Syndicate	....	....	....
,,	....	....	....
,,	....	....	....
,,	....	....	....
,,	....	....	....
,,	....	....	....

(b) The following profits (as defined at Part III Para. 2 (d) of Lloyd's Circular dated..........................) were paid or credited to the Member in respect of the 19.......... account closed 31 December 19.............

	No.	*Amount*
Syndicate	....	....
,,		....
,,	....	....
,,	....	....
,,	....	....
,,	....	....

Signature..

Name and address of
Underwriting Agent..

....

Date..

LL 20

Appendix 5

TELEGRAPHIC ADDRESS:
LLOYDS LONDON EC3
TELEX: 987321 LLOYDS G
TELEPHONE: 01 623 7100
INTERNATIONAL: + 44 1 623 7100
EXTENSION: 3828
OUR REFERENCE:— 3455R

LLOYD'S
LONDON HOUSE,
6 LONDON STREET,
LONDON,
EC3R 7AB.
30th August, 1985

Dear Sir(s)

US & Canadian Tax Credit Relief for Lloyd's Names

The present method of computing US tax credit relief requires the income and tax shown in the Names' US tax returns to be allocated over the relevant four underwriting years of account; e.g. the 1984 return would include the 1981 account Underwriting profit or loss and the 1984 calendar year investment income allocated to account years 1982, 1983 and 1984.

It can be seen therefore that each US tax return impacts on four UK years of assessment. This complication is troublesome enough in itself but when net operating losses are carried back, for up to 3 years, such carry back can result in the reopening of up to six previous UK years of assessment.

The number of US net operating loss carry-backs has risen significantly in recent years to the extent that the resources at Leeds (Underwriters Unit) were in danger of becoming inadequate to deal with the volume of work.

In an attempt to alleviate this problem it was decided to simplify the basis upon which US tax credit relief is calculated. Accordingly a series of dicussions took place between Leeds (Underwriters Unit), Lloyd's Underwriting Agents Association Tax Liaison Group and Taxation Department. A new basis has been formulated which has received the approval of the Board of Inland Revenue and which has been agreed by the LUAA and the Committee of Lloyd's. The new basis will not only reduce the amount of work for Names, their accountants and this Department it will also ease the reconciliation between the tax shown by the US return and the UK tax credit relief given.

The details of the new basis are set out in the attached memorandum (appendix A) and the formal agreement with the Inland Revenue is included as appendix B. A provisional sample of the Tax Credit Relief Report which will be produced by Taxation Department is included as appendix C. Although the final version of the report may vary from this in minor details of format, it is likely to be very similar in all essentials.

I would draw your attention particularly to Clause 7 of the Agreement which permits any Underwriter to opt out of the new arrangements but, having done so, he will not be permitted to opt in again. It is our firm belief that these new arrangements are of great benefit to Names and their Accountants and there would seem to be little or no benefit to a Name in opting out. It has to be understood that if a Name does opt out it will be up to him or his accountant to provide the necessary year of account apportionments without any assistance from Taxation Dept. Under the new system these apportionments will not be maintained on Lloyd's computer system.

Some adjustments to the tax credit relief calculations will arise from the Finance Act 1985 legislation as it applies to Lloyd's. These adjustments are explained in appendix D to this letter.

This letter is being sent to all Underwriting Agents and Panel auditors.

Yours Faithfully,

Manager
Taxation Department

Appendix A: Simplified basis of US and Canadian Tax Credit Relief

General Principles

The essence of the simplification is that, instead of allocating the US tax to Underwriting years of account, it will be advised to Leeds (Underwriters Unit) by Lloyd's Taxation Department on a calendar year basis. Canadian tax is currently computed on an Underwriting Account basis so that the Lloyd's Canadian tax credit system will require little change. The calendar year data provided by Taxation Department will show, on an individual Name basis, the US and Canadian tax broken down to the following categories:

      Case I   :   Underwriting profit/loss
      Case IV :   Investment income
      Case VI :   Investment income
      Capital gains
      Personal, Non-Lloyd's (US tax only)

The first year to which the new system will apply is the 1984 US tax year and Leeds (Underwriters Unit) will apply this tax to the UK 1983/84 Assessment (1983 Underwriting Account). Leeds (Underwriters Unit) will deal with the 1984 US tax returns (filed on 15th June 1985) at the same time as the 1985 Canadian Tax Returns (filed on 15th April 1986). Taxation Department will provide figures, on an individual Name basis, for US & Canadian tax on simultaneous reports. The total US and Canadian tax will be shown in both dollars and sterling, the breakdown to income categories in sterling only. The rates of exchange used will be the same as those used under the present system. The reports will show the country of residence of the Name. Names whose US returns are not filed by LeBoeuf, Lamb, Leiby & MacRae (whether US Names or not) will have Canadian tax reported only.

Copies of the reports will be supplied to Names, via their co-ordinating agent.

Under the present system Leeds (Underwriters Unit) forwards to each Name a claim form based on the tax credit relief figures provided by Taxation Department. The Name is required to return this form to Leeds (Underwriters Unit) before receiving relief. Under the new system Names will make the claim on the basis of the figures on their copy of the report and Leeds (Underwriters Unit) will *not* send them a claim form. Names will be entitled to claim tax credit relief on 1st January one year after the close of the Underwriting Account to which the UK Assessment applies i.e. 1984 tax applied to 1983/84 assessment (1983 Underwriting account closed December 1985). Therefore relief for the 1984 US tax will be repayable to UK resident Names after 1st January 1987. Where possible, claims should be submitted at the same time as those for Case I loss relief and capital gains repayment. Tax credit relief claims need not be submitted for non-resident Names as relief will be granted by deduction against the 1983 Underwriting results. The effect of this timing is that the whole of the 1984 US tax will be eligible for tax credit relief on 1st January 1987, whereas under the old system the 1981 and 1982 Account proportion of the 1984 tax would have been relieved in the Summer of 1986, the 1983 Account proportion in 1987 and the 1984 Account proportion in 1988.

Net Operating Losses

Refunds of tax from NOL's will be advised to Leeds (Underwriters Unit) by Taxation Department and will be allocated to the five categories, Case I, Case IV, Case VI, Capital gains and personal income.

Reductions of tax credit relief on account of net operating losses will be incorporated in the Tax Credit Relief Reports for the year in which the net operating losses arose. Leeds (Underwriters Unit) will offset the tax credit relief without referral to the tax credit relief previously given (unless tax credit relief has been restricted for "E" cases). Thus some excess tax credit relief may be reclaimed. To compensate for this disadvantage to Names Leeds (Underwriters Unit) will not reclaim repayment supplement paid on the tax credit relief previously given.

If a Name insists on net operating losses being handled on the statutory basis i.e. referring to the tax credit relief previously given and having that amount only reclaimed, Leeds (Underwriters Unit) will also reclaim the repayment supplement.

When reporting NOL refunds, Taxation Department will show the refund of tax on the three separate years to which the NOL was carried and will convert the tax refunded at the rate of exchange used when refund of the original tax was advised to Leeds (Underwriters Unit). Each year's refund of tax will be broken down to the five categories and then totalled.

Amended Returns

When amended returns are filed in future (other than net operating loss cases) the resulting refund or additional tax will be allocated to the five categories and shown on the Taxation Department report. Leeds (Underwriters Unit) will either relieve the additional tax or reclaim the refund. Where such an amended return affects other returns by altering the Name's available net operating loss, each such other returns will be treated as a separate amended returns as distinct from the treatment given to original net operating losses as set out above.

Non-LeBoeuf Names

Names, for whom LeBoeuf, Lamb, Leiby & MacRae do not file US tax returns, and US citizens resident in the UK may also move to the new basis if they so wish but they should contact Leeds (Underwriters Unit) to confirm their intention to do so.

Transitional Problems

The Double Tax Relief Reports for US Tax year 1983 prepared under the old system have been forwarded to Leeds (Underwriters Unit) and the 1981 account element of the investment income & capital gains is being relieved during 1985. This will leave income & capital gains for 1982 account (included in the 1982 & 1983 returns) and for 1983 account (included in 1983 returns) unrelieved. Leeds (Underwriters Unit) will relieve these items against income from 1982 Underwriting Account and repayments will be made during 1986.

Opting Out of the New Basis

It was accepted that if a Name objected to the change and insisted on his case being handled under the old principles he should be free to do so. Therefore Names may elect to opt out of the new basis, such election to be made in writing to Leeds (Underwriters Unit). Once made the election is irrevocable. Names who so elect will have to provide for themselves the breakdown of US income and tax to the respective years of account because Lloyd's system will no longer be able to do so.

Method of making claims for tax credit relief
Transitional years

> 1982 US Return, 1982 Account element
> 1983 US Return, 1982 and 1983 Account elements

These will be repaid by Leeds (Underwriters Unit) early in 1986 using the existing method i.e. Leeds (Underwriters Unit) will send out forms to Names and request a claim.

Canadian tax 1984 has already been relieved with US tax 1983—1981 Account.

US tax year 1984 and Canadian tax year 1985
This tax will be set against UK tax of 1983 Underwriting Account, 1983/4 UK year of assessment (and later years similarly). No request for claim will be sent by Leeds (Underwriters Unit) but UK Names must submit their own claim on the basis of the Lloyd's Taxation Department Tax Credit Relief Reports and supporting vouchers (Forms LL185E).

NB. Vouchers are not required for relief against capital gains tax. Hitherto accrued income has been treated as a capital item and not vouched. Henceforth vouchers will be required for accrued income. Leeds (Underwriters Unit) would have no objection to including both Case IV income and Case VI income on the same voucher.

Claims will be admitted after 1st January 1987 and it is suggested that Names claim tax credit relief at the same time as the annual claims in respect of capital gains repayment and Case I loss relief.

Non-residents of the UK need not make a claim because Leeds (Underwriters Unit) will show a deduction for US and Canadian tax on the Form LL9.

Personal income
Leeds (Underwriters Unit) will not give relief for tax on personal income—this will be the responsibility of the Names' Main Tax District.

Where net operating losses have been applied to personal income it will be up to the Main District to reclaim the excess tax credit relief. Leeds (Underwriters Unit) will advise Main Districts of cases where such amounts are substantial.

Deceased and Resigned Names
There is a problem in the last two tax years because there will be no UK assessment year to which to apply the US and Canadian tax e.g:

Name resigned 31st December 1985—last U/wg. Account 1985
US Tax Return 1987 should apply to Account 1986
US Tax Return 1988 should apply to Account 1987 (Case I only)
Canadian Tax Return 1988 should apply to Account 1986

Leeds (Underwriters Unit) will apply the US and Canadian tax to the last two UK years of assessment i.e. to 1985 and 1984. If still not fully relieved it will then be applied to the previous two years 1983 and 1982. By this means it is expected that all the tax will be relieved. To cover this eventuality Accountants should ensure that all vouchers are sent to Leeds (Underwriters Unit) for the last four years of a deceased or resigned Name rather than just those sufficient to cover the US and Canadian tax.

The problem should not apply to deceased Names who participate in the Estate Protection Plan (or similar approved plans) because the foreign tax will be met out of income which has suffered no UK tax. Recoveries made under the Plan will be net of foreign tax paid and the Estate will therefore have received relief by deduction but not tax credit relief. If assessable recoveries are received from the Plan foreign tax allowed by deduction will be added to the amount assessable and full tax credit relief given in terms of tax against the assessed liabilities.

New Names
Due to the interplay of tax years and underwriting years under the new system a new Name in his first US tax year will not have a Lloyd's UK assessment year to which to apply the US tax. (i.e. New Name 1984, 1984 US tax should be applied to 1983 Account).

Therefore Leeds (Underwriters Unit) will hold the 1984 US tax until the 1985 US tax has been reported and apply both to the 1984 Account. If this results in restriction of tax credit relief because of insufficient UK tax on 1984 Account, the unrelieved portion will be carried forward to the next two UK years.

Appendix B: Simplified system for granting tax credit relief for Lloyd's Names

Agreement between Lloyd's & Inland Revenue

1. The new system is to operate for relief relating to the Lloyd's Underwriting Year 1983, closed 31 December 1985.

2. Tax Credit Relief for that year is to be based on tax paid on the 1984 US Tax Return and the 1985 Canadian Return. There is to be no re-allocation of Foreign Tax between more than one Lloyd's Underwriting Years.

3. For the US tax year 1984 and the Canadian tax year 1985, Lloyd's will produce a printout for each Underwriter involved

setting out his Name and Membership Number, the country of residence and the amounts of tax paid split between Case I, Case IV, Case VI, Capital Gains and non-Lloyd's personal income. In addition, this printout will include the net operating loss liabilities for 1984 converted into sterling.

4. Copies of the printout will be sent to Leeds (Underwriters Unit) by June 1986 with a further copy sent at the same time to the Names' co-ordinating agents for onward transmission to the personal accountants. Relief will be repayable to UK resident Names after 1 January 1987 when the tax for Lloyd's Underwriting Year 1983 becomes due and payable. Where possible, claims should be submitted at the same time as those for Case I loss relief and Capital Gains repayment.

Tax Credit Relief claims need not be submitted for non-resident Names as relief will be granted by deduction against the 1983 Underwriting results.

5. Net operating liabilities for the United States year 1984 and the Canadian year 1985 will be deducted from repayments of tax credit relief for Account 1983, with any balance of such liabilities deducted from the next repayment due. The calculation of net operating liabilities under the streamlined system will ignore over-repaid supplement. Where a repayment of tax credit relief for Lloyd's underwriting years 1980 and 1981 has been restricted because of the use of estimated figures in arriving at Case I profits or losses, any over-repayment will be restricted to the amount actually repaid.

6. Amounts of Foreign Tax relating to United States Returns before the first Returns coming into the new system, which have not yet been relieved, will all be relieved against income from Lloyd's Underwriting Year 1982 and repayments will be made during 1986.

7. Any Underwriter who does not wish to take part in these arrangements will be required to formulate his own claim and submit it to Leeds (Underwriters Unit). Recalculations will also be required for net operating liabilities and the concession on supplement will not be available. In respect of the 1984 United States and 1985 Canadian Returns an election to opt out of the arrangements should be made to Leeds (Underwriters Unit) as soon as possible. Once a Name has opted out of the new system, he will not be allowed to opt in again for a future year and it will not be possible to cancel an election to opt out once it has been made.

8. Names not using the LeBoeuf Lamb arrangements to file Returns in the United States will be able to opt into the new tax credit relief system, and provide manual calculations on a calendar year basis—i.e. 1984 US tax to be claimed after 1 January 1987 against the Account 1983 Lloyd's results, with unrelieved elements from the 1982 and 1983 US Returns being claimed after 1 January 1986.

9. New Names will have paid US tax on two years investment income and Capital Gains before their first Lloyd's results are charged in the United Kingdom. Where possible Tax Credit Relief will be granted for both US Years against the first United Kingdom result, but where there is insufficient tax to cover both, unrelieved balances from the second United States Return will be carried forward and allowed against the next United Kingdom results. A similar exercise will be applied, where necessary, to the following year's results, but no further carry forward of unrelieved US tax will be permitted beyond the third Lloyd's account.

10. For deceased and resigned Names, where underwriting results are not covered by the terms of a reinsurance or quota share policy, two United States Returns and one Canadian Return will be left unrelieved. Credit for these amounts will be vouched from the penultimate and final United Kingdom results to which they relate. Where insufficient tax remains in charge in those years, unrelieved amounts will be vouched against the two earlier account results, but no further carry back will then be permitted. Tax Credit Relief for results covered by a reinsurance or quota share plan will be viewed at the time recoveries made under the terms of such a policy are being assessed.

Appendix C: Lloyd's double tax relief report

US TAX 1985: CANADIAN TAX 1986: UK YEAR OF ASSESSMENT 1984/85

MEMBERS COPY

MEMBER'S CODE: 12346A
MEMBER'S NAME: SMITH J J

CO-ORDINATING AGENT: 1234B

COUNTRY OF RESIDENCE: UNITED KINGDOM

	EXCHANGE RATE	TOTAL $	TOTAL £	UNDERWRITING PROFIT/LOSS (CASE 1) £	INVESTMENT INCOME (CASE 4) £	ACCRUED INTEREST (CASE 6) £	CAPITAL GAINS £	LLOYD'S TOTAL £	NON-LLOYD'S (PERSONAL) £
US TAX									
ORIGINAL TAX / NOL TAX REDUCTION 1985	1.33	2000	1500.75	0.00	600.30	450.20	300.15	1350.65	150.10
1984	1.20	(300)	(250.00)	0.00	(150.00)	(30.00)	(40.00)	(220.00)	(30.00)
1983	1.36	180	110.00	(88.00)	16.50	6.50	0.00	110.00	0.00
1982	1.25	250	200.00	(100.00)	40.00	20.00	20.00	180.00	20.00
SUB TOTAL		1300	940.75	(188.00)	393.80	394.70	240.15	840.65	100.10
ADJUSTMENTS FOR AMENDED RETURNS 1984	1.20	(300)	(250.00)	(0.00)	(150.00)	(30.00)	(40.00)	(220.00)	(30.00)
1983	1.36	250	170.00	136.00	25.50	8.50	0.00	170.00	0.00
NET US TCR DUE OR (EXCESS TCR GIVEN)		1250	860.75	(52.00)	289.30	373.20	200.15	790.65	70.10
CANADIAN TAX									
ORIGINAL TAX 1986	1.76	1500	850.00	300.25	250.75	175.20	124.30	850.50	
NET TOTAL TCR DUE OR (EXCESS TCR GIVEN)			1711.25	248.25	520.05	548.40	324.45	1641.15	70.10

NOTE TO AGENT: This report is to be forwarded immediately to the Name's personal accountant or, if the accountant not known, to the Name.

NOTE FOR MEMBERS:
1. A copy of this report has been sent to Leeds (Underwriters Unit).
2. Claims for tax credit relief must be made by Names to Leeds (Underwriters Unit) together with forms LL185E.
   Claims will not be admitted until 1st January next.
3. A claim is not required from non-resident Names as relief will be given automatically by deduction.
   This will appear on the next form LL9.
4. Claims for TCR on personal (non-Lloyd's) income, if any, must be made through the Name's main tax office.
5. Where a Name's tax refunds shown on the report exceed the tax liabilities ie. the total line "NET TCR DUE OR (EXCESS TCR GIVEN)" is negative this excess will be collected by Leeds (Underwriters Unit) from the next repayment made.

Appendix D: Finance Act 1985—bondwashing adjustments

The Finance Act provisions applying to Lloyd's require that accrued income received on or after 1st January 1986 is to be treated as Case VI income and not capital gain.

Due to the way calendar year investment income is Riescoed at Lloyd's some mismatching arises; e.g.:

The 1984 Account investment income arises in calendar years 1984, 1985 and 1986. Therefore some 1984 Account investment income will arise before and some after 1st January 1986. However, under the new basis of tax credit relief, the US tax on investment income of calendar year 1985 will be applied to UK Account year 1984. It will be seen therefore that the US accrued income of calendar year 1985 must be divided as between the amount to be treated as capital and the amount treated as Case VI income. If this were not done and, say, the accrued income was advised to Leeds (Underwriters Unit) as 100% capital, the Name would probably have insufficient UK capital gains tax to which to apply the US tax on capital.

Average Riesco percentages, agreed with the Inland Revenue, will be used to so apportion the accrued income included in US tax returns for 1985 & 1986 and Canadian tax returns for 1986 & 1987. The averages taken for this purpose are 15%, 25% and 60%.

New Names pose a problem because their first year's US tax does not have a relevant Lloyd's UK assessment year. Therefore in their first year New Names 1984 and 1985 will have different percentages applied to their accrued income i.e.:

New Name 1984
US Tax 1984 will be related to 1984 A/c—40% Capital gain
US Tax 1985 will relate to   1984 A/c—40% Capital gain
US Tax 1986 will relate to   1985 A/c—15% Capital gain

New Name 1985
US Tax 1985 will be related to 1985 A/c—15% Capital gain
US Tax 1986 will relate to   1985 A/c—15% Capital gain

This is not a problem for new Names' Canadian tax because Canadian tax returns are filed on an account year basis. Thus 1985 Canadian tax returns include 1982 account income and the 1985 tax can be related to 1983/4 UK assessment for all Names.

The following table shows the application of the percentages to the US and Canadian tax years:

CALENDAR YEAR

1983   1984   1985 | 1986   1987   1988

Accrued income
Treated as capital

Accrued income
Treated as income

A/C year

1983   15% 25% 60%

1984   15% 25% | 60%

1985   15% | 25% | 60%

1986 | 15% | 25% | 60% |

| US TAX YEAR | CANADIAN | | RELATED TO UK ACCOUNT | UK ASSESSMENT YEAR | % OF ACCR AS CAPITAL (US & CAN) | % CAPITAL FOR NEW NAMES (US ONLY) |
	TAX YEAR	A/C YEAR				
1984	1985	1982	1983	1983/4	100%	40%
1985	1986	1983	1984	1984/5	40%	15%
1986	1987	1984	1985	1985/6	15%	0
1987	1988	1985	1986	1986/7	0	0

Appendix 6

Memorandum from the Capital Taxes Office: Valuations for capital transfer tax

The rates used for discounting purposes are currently as follows:

	Current Valuation Cases involving deaths before 1.9.82	*Deaths on and after 1.9.82*
1. Lloyd's Audit Basis		
Deposits and Reserves (simple)	$3\frac{1}{2}$ per annum*	$3\frac{1}{2}$ per annum*
Profits (discount tables)	7% per annum	6% per annum
Losses (discount tables)	4% per annum	4% per annum
2. Acutal Basis (which is concessionary)		
Deposits and Reserves	$3\frac{1}{2}$ (as above)*	$3\frac{1}{2}$ per annum
Profits	14% per annum	12% per annum
Losses	14% *less* the mean of	12% (*less* same adjustment formula)

Yields on $2\frac{1}{2}$% Consols and the FT All Shares Index net of tax.

(*from date of death to estimated date of release and subject to a maximum discount of 10%).

Possibly an easier way of illustrating the discounts applied by this Division, upon actuarial advice, is by way of an imaginary case and by adding relevant footnotes:

A Name deceased
died 1.10.81

(Pre 1.9.82 valuation formula)

A. Open Year
   Accounts*1

Syndicates	1979 a/c*2	1980 a/c*3	1981 a/c*2
1	500	250	1,750
2	750	(1,000)	(250)
3	(250)	(1,500)	150
	1,000*3	(2,250)*3	1,650*3

$1,000 \times [V\ ^3/_4 *4 \times 7\% *5 = .9505]*6 = 950$
$(2,250) \times [V1^3/_4 \times 4\% *7 = .9337] = (2,100)$
$1,650 \times [V2^3/_4 \times 7\% = .8302] = \underline{1,370}$

220

B. Deposits and Reserves

Investments	=	35,000
Less dividends =		(250)
Secured Bank Guarantee*9	=	15,000
		49,750

Less 9.625 discount*10 (x.90375) 44.962

45,182

Less 50% Business relief*11 (x.50 = £22,591 (Value for Capital Transfer Tax).

Notes
*1. The basis of valuation is section 38 of the Finance Act 1975, the successor to section 7(5) of the Finance Act 1894. (See also paragraph 2(2)(a) Schedule 4 of the Finance Act 1975.)

On the strict statutory basis the Lloyd's Audit basis of valuation should apply. However by concession the legal personal representatives are allowed to elect within 12 months from the date of grant for the actual result for the open years. Where the option is not exercised the Lloyd's Audit basis of valuation will automatically apply.

In cases where Deeds of Family Arrangement are executed after 10 months from the date of grant and which make the Underwriting Interest taxable for the first time, the usual practice is to allow the LPRs 2 months to elect from the date of this Division's initial letter.

*2. Latest at date of death Lloyd's Audit figures used. In this particular example this will be the Lloyd's Audit figures as at 31st December 1980 for the 1979 and 1980 accounts and the LA figures as at 31st December 1981 for the 1981 accounts.

In Actual valuations we adopt the final accounts figures, after adding back any foreign taxation which is treated as a separate asset/liability of the estate, which in this example should close 31st December 1981, 1982 and 1983 respectively.

*3. In Lloyd's Audit valuations only, where the death occurs in the first 6 months of the year the earliest open account (ie in this case the 1979 account) is discounted by 5% and the subsequent open years (ie the 1980 and 1981 accounts) are discounted by $7\frac{1}{2}$%. Profits thereby decrease and losses in respect of this first discount, increase.

*4. Estimated period to settlement (eg the 1979 account should close 31st December 1981 and be settled in approximately mid 1982 which is $\frac{3}{4}$ of a year after the date of death).

*5. Standard discount given on profits for Lloyd's Audit valuations. In actual valuations profits discounted by 14% per annum.

*6. Discount factor using 'Parry's valuation and conversion tables' using the table for 'years purchase (dual rate—without allowance for tax)' on the estimated period from the date of death to the date of payment.

*7. Standard discount given on losses for Lloyd's Audit valuations. In Actual valuations losses discounted by the mean of the yield on $2\frac{1}{2}$% Consolidated Stock and the Financial Times All Shares Index—both at the date of death—net of tax, deducted from 14% and the resulting figure rounded up.

*8. Dividends paid after the date of death on investments quoted ex dividend at the date of death are treated as part of the deceased's general free estate. Accrued interest on short dated government stocks is however included as part of the value of the Underwriting interest.

*9. The value of Bank Guarantees—or the value of the underlying security if this is less—are treated as part of the Underwriting Interest provided such security is subject under the guarantee to normal constraints on user. (See also 11, below).

*10. Discount to Deposits and Reserves given at the straight rate of $3\frac{1}{2}\%$ per annum—subject to a maximum discount of 10%—from date of death to estimated *final* settlement date. (ie $2\frac{3}{4} \times 3\frac{1}{2}\% = 9.625\%$). The reason for this lower rate is due to the fact that during the winding up period the estate continues to enjoy the benefit of the income/capital appreciation from the underlying investments.

*11. Business Relief given under the provisions of the Finance Act 1976, Schedule 10 as amended by section 64 of the Finance Act 1978 on the discounted value of the Deposits and Reserves after adding/deducting the net discounted value of the *open* (but not the closed) year's account. Note in the case of Bank Guarantees secured upon Agricultural property Business Relief is not allowed where Agricultural relief has been given: Finance Act 1976, Schedule 10, paragraph 10.

Although I have endeavoured in the above comments to show this Division's valuation formula—which has been successfully applied in recent years to the mutual benefit of both sides—as clear as possible, as I trust you will appreciate this Division reserves the right to adjust any of the rates without prior consultation. Further this Division will not of course be bound by any inaccuracy which may have occurred in the above notes.

Index of statutes

Index